Searching for ANSWERS

the Unquenchable Thirst

Searching for ANSWERS

the Unquenchable Thirst

BRITTON WEIMER
PAUL JOHNSON

God's Word is our highest calling.

Searching For Answers: The Unquenchable Thirst

Published by AMG Publishers
6815 Shallowford Rd.
Chattanooga, Tennessee 37421

ISBN 0-89957-356-8

First printing—January 2003

Cover designed by The Williams Company, Chattanooga, Tennessee
Interior design and typesetting by Reider Publishing Services, West Hollywood, California
Edited and Proofread by Tricia Toney, Dan Penwell, and Jody El-Assadi

Printed in Canada
09 08 07 06 05 04 03 –T– 8 7 6 5 4 3 2 1

We dedicate this book to our wives—Judy and Darla—
whose affection, encouragement, and inquisitiveness
greatly inspired the book!

Contents

Acknowledgments

WE ARE INDEBTED to the many people who helped us write this book. Marilyn Bowman, John Eichenlaub, Fred Overdier, and Ruth Overdier were kind enough to wade through the entire manuscript, offering invaluable suggestions and encouragement.

In addition, several people read individual chapters and generally helped us to sharpen the concepts in the book. These include: David Clark, Patrick Hawkins, Miles Mahaffey, Kevin Meyer, Richard Meyers, Noelle Roso, David Weimer, and Mark Weimer.

Other friends and family too numerous to name have helped and encouraged us throughout the many years we have worked on this project. They patiently listened to and improved the "great ideas" we wanted to put into the book.

Finally, we are grateful for the excellent editorial work by Tricia Toney and Jody El-Assadi, the wonderful page design and typesetting of Andrea Reider, and the oversight of the complete project from editorial to completion by Dan Penwell.

Introduction

"IF A GOOD God exists, why is there evil in the world?" This question has perplexed morally serious people throughout human history. Sixteen centuries ago, it was a question that haunted a brilliant young African, Aurelius Augustinus.

Augustinus was born into the powerful and cosmopolitan Roman Empire. His family was prosperous, and he was sheltered from many of life's hardships. Yet he was a sensitive soul, disturbed by the sufferings of others.

Although Augustinus' father was irreligious, his mother was a devout Christian. As a child he had accepted his mother's faith, but he discarded it as a teenager. He found the Christian Bible crude and unsophisticated, when compared to eloquent Latin writers like Cicero. Moreover, he did not believe Christianity addressed the problem of evil.

Augustinus was initially drawn to the Manichean philosophy, which claimed to solve the problem of evil. According to Manicheism, and to most other religions and philosophies in Roman times, evil is inherent in matter. Only God and the human soul are morally good. A degenerate being had created the material realm; God had not created it. God was separate from the universe, and not responsible for its evil. This separation appeared to solve the problem of evil, absolving God from responsibility.

However, Augustinus ultimately found the Manichean solution unsatisfactory. It made people morally careless about everyday life. If the natural world is evil, then our interactions with the natural world cannot be morally good. Yet, Augustinus recognized, most of our lives are spent interacting with the natural world.

On a practical level, then, Manicheism led to moral anarchy and to rampant rationalizing of selfish behavior. Augustinus himself fell into that trap. He devoted himself to pleasure, took a mistress, and had a son outside of marriage.

The Manichean philosophy had "solved" the problem of evil by trivializing it. By limiting evil to the external world, it had shifted moral responsibility away from people. The real problem, Augustinus finally concluded, is in the human heart. People are slaves to self-interest—a moral flaw not one of the Roman religions or philosophies could cure.

Augustinus then took a fresh look at the faith of his childhood. Perhaps he had misjudged Christianity? Perhaps the simplicity and directness of the Christian Bible was a virtue, not a flaw? Perhaps it contained a realistic solution to the problem of evil, in language understandable to the average person?

Augustinus carefully studied the Christian Bible, and concluded it squarely addressed the problem of evil. The problem was indeed in the human heart, not in the material world or other convenient scapegoats. Human selfishness caused evil. God was not the source, but He did provide a way of escape.

Today we know Augustinus as Saint Augustine. His conversion to Christianity is recorded in a classic autobiographical work, *The Confessions*. *The Confessions* is considered by many modern scholars to be the first modern autobiography, and a precursor to modern psychology.

Augustine was a brilliant thinker, but was he correct? Does the Christian Bible truly solve the problem of human evil? Is the Christian solution substantially different from other world religions? In this book, we make a humble effort to answer these questions.

The authors of this book believe that Christianity does uniquely solve the problem of evil. However, we also believe that the Christian solution is reasonable and logical. We believe it can stand on its own, without the reader having to first accept the accuracy of the Christian Scriptures.

Thus, as you read the book, you will see that we do not rely upon the Christian Bible to make our case. Instead, we seek to use a wide range of non-Christian thinkers and sources. As much as possible, we have focused on thinkers who have not been influenced by Christianity—by ancient thinkers before the time of Christ—Eastern religions and philosophers, "primitive religions," and modern scientists. Hopefully you will find that we have been objective and accurate in our research and in our analysis.

There is a logical progression in the chapters of this book. As you read, you may disagree with a particular chapter's basic conclusions. If so, we encourage you to stop at that point and do your own research. At the end of each chapter we provide options for further reading, and you will have no trouble finding other sources on the basic questions in this book. After further study, if you are "on track" with the book, then we encourage you to keep reading.

This book has a simple premise. The human race has a practical need. We have violated the moral law, and need forgiveness. We have a great moral thirst, one that cannot be quenched by ordinary means. We cannot be happy or free until this thirst is acknowledged and satisfied.

Under any standard religious framework, though, this thirst appears to be unquenchable. Neither good works nor religious ritual is satisfactory. Both, to be effective, would require God to leave immoral acts unpunished.

Is our moral thirst in fact unquenchable? Is forgiveness impossible? Has any religion truly solved this problem? Can any religion quench this universal thirst?

Join us as we explore this vital question. Follow in the footsteps of the world's greatest thinkers. See what they discover about God and humanity. Then evaluate the power of world religions to address the universal dilemma—the eternal conflict between human nature and the moral law.

I

Does God Exist?

PAUL DAVIES is professor of mathematical physics at the University of Adelaide in Australia. He has an international reputation for his wide-ranging research into basic principles of physics and cosmology.

Davies has closely examined the most basic question of all—whether God created the universe. In the early 1980s, Davies was agnostic. He focused on cosmological theories that could eliminate the need for a Creator. In particular, he noted that there could be multiple universes, and our universe could simply be a spin-off from another, older universe.[1]

However, Davies was not satisfied with his own explanations. He probed more deeply. Perhaps there are an infinite number of universes. But then the same physical laws would govern them all.

What Davies found was right in front of him. These physical laws are so predictable and simple that they can be defined by mathematics. "Few scientists stop to wonder why the fundamental laws of the universe are mathematical," he noted. Most just "take it for granted."[2]

Without rational laws, no universe could exist; all would be chaos. Moreover, without our *particular* physical laws, *human life* could not exist. Science provides "impressive evidence" that life "depends very sensitively on the form of the laws of physics." Scientists have discovered a long list of "lucky accidents" and "coincidences" in the specific values assigned to various particles and forces, all of which are essential to human survival.[3]

What is the source of these rational, mathematical laws? Davies could not shake this basic question. Finally, he concluded that there is only one reasonable explanation. Nature's laws imply an intelligent law-giving Creator. To know these laws, then, is to know the "mind of God."

Davies is not alone. Throughout history, from tribal religions to modern science, inquisitive people have concluded that the Creation requires a Creator.

Native American Great Spirit

Approximately 10,000 B.C.E., Asian tribes migrated across the frozen Bering Strait into North America. They were the ancestors of today's Native Americans. These tribes have maintained their beliefs and traditions, largely unchanged, for thousands of years.

Despite their distinct cultures, most Native Americans held certain religious beliefs in common. Most associated gods with the forces of nature, gods who must be appeased in crises such as drought and disease. Significantly, most also believed that there is a Great Spirit who is superior to the particular gods of nature.

For example, the Delaware Indians occupied a large area from Ontario southward into Oklahoma. They believed in Gicelemu Kaong, which translated means "Great Spirit" or "Creator." He is the leader of all other gods, who are his agents to control the forces of nature. He created the earth and everything in it. On special occasions, with much ceremony, the Delaware would pray to the Great Spirit, giving thanks for his benefits. However, these prayers required great effort. The Great Spirit lives in the twelfth heaven (or highest heaven) above the earth, and it takes twelve shouts or cries to reach his ears. Therefore, the Delaware worship was ordinarily directed to the lesser gods, who are much more accessible.[4]

Similar ancient beliefs in a Great Spirit have been documented among many other tribes. To the Hopi, he was known as Taiowa.[5] To the Dakota, he was Wankan Tanka; to the Pawnee, he was Tirawa.[6] To the Omaha, he was Wakonda.[7] He was the inaccessible Creator, the Ruler over all the gods of nature.

Ptah-Hetep (3000 B.C.E.)

At the beginning of their civilization, the Egyptians believed in a supreme Creator, Neter.[8] He was self-existent and immortal.[9] He was superior to all other Egyptian gods, including their sun god, Ra.[10]

The Egyptian sage Ptah-Hetep is a classic representative of this early Egyptian belief in one superior God. He composed his *Precepts* about 3000 B.C.E., when the Great Pyramid was still a new building. His *Precepts* encompassed "the whole duty of man" to God and society.[11]

Ptah-Hetep taught that all people, both small and great, are accountable to God. The humble farmer must farm with diligence: "If you have ground to till, labor in the field which God has given you."[12] The mighty are also accountable: "If you have become governor of the city, be not hard-hearted on account of your advancement, because you have become merely the guardian of the things which God has provided."[13]

As Egypt grew older, though, its religious focus shifted away from Neter. Instead, Egyptians emphasized subordinate gods such as the sun god, Ra.

Aristotle (384 – 322 B.C.E.)

Aristotle was born in Macedon, Greece. His father, Nicomachus, was the court physician to the Macedonian king. Through his father, Aristotle was introduced to medicine and biology at an early age.

Nicomachus died when Aristotle was seventeen, and his family sent him to Plato's Academy in Athens. He remained there for twenty years, first as a student, then as a teacher, gaining renown for his mastery of rhetoric.

After leaving the Academy, Aristotle helped establish a new school in Asia Minor, focusing on political theory. He married, had a son, and had a happy family life. During this time, Aristotle also tutored the young Alexander the Great.

Thereafter, Aristotle returned to Athens and founded a school, the Lyceum, where he taught for many years. He was convinced that the universe is rational, and that its order can be discovered through observation and logical analysis. Based upon this conviction, he made the Lyceum into a major research center, specializing in empirical sciences such as biology, zoology, and history.

Beyond his work as a teacher, Aristotle produced an astonishing output of writing on almost every conceivable field of knowledge—logic, ethics, history, metaphysics, politics, rhetoric, biology, poetry, psychology, physics, and zoology. In most cases, his writings were so advanced and encyclopedic that they dominated western thinking until the rise of modern science.

Aristotle's relentless logic can be clearly seen in his study of metaphysics. Aristotle observed that every effect in the universe has a cause. What do we find if we trace those causes back in time?

Aristotle rejected the idea that there is an "infinite regress" of causes, going back into eternity past.[14] Such a view is inconsistent with the order and design in the universe.

Instead, there must be an intelligent God, the First Cause or Unmoved Mover outside of the universe. Only God is "infinite" and "eternal." Only God can "move without being moved." Thus, only God is capable of starting the universe's chain of causation.[15]

Aristotle's argument for the Unmoved Mover remains a powerful argument, even in today's scientific culture. Though not proving God's existence absolutely, it demonstrates the probability that God is the universe's First Cause.

Traditional African High God

Prior to the arrival of Christianity, most African tribes were outwardly polytheistic. They focused on appeasing local deities thought to control the forces of nature.

Behind this polytheism, though, was a widespread African belief in a supreme God—a High God superior to the local gods. This High God was the Creator, all-powerful, and morally pure. However, He was removed from humanity and inaccessible for most practical purposes.

For example, the Bakongo tribe is native to the lower Congo River area. They worship Nzambi Mpungu, the God who made all people and all things. He creates every child, punishes evil, and removes the soul at the hour of death. He is the unapproachable sovereign Master. The Bakongo render him no worship, for he has need of none.[16]

Similarly, the Isoko tribe in southern Nigeria acknowledges Cghene. He is the Supreme Being, who created the world and all people. He punishes evil and rewards good. He lives in the sky, is invisible, and is beyond human comprehension. Cghene is so distant and unknowable that he has no temples or priests, and no direct prayers or sacrifices are offered to him.[17]

This High God was (and is) recognized throughout Africa, by tribes originally separated by barriers of geography, language, and culture. To the Kikuyu of East Africa, he is Ngai; to the Baila of Northern Rhodesia, he is Leza. To the Herero of Southwest Africa, he is Ndjambi; to the Venda of the Northern Transvaal, he is Raluvhimba.[18] In each case, he is too distant, powerful, and good to be troubled except in great crises.[19]

Kepler (1571–1630)

Modern science is built on a monotheistic foundation. Western thinkers were convinced that God created the universe, and governs it by law. The laws of this rational universe can be discovered by experimentation, and defined by mathematics.

A premier example of this God-based confidence in natural law was Johannes Kepler, the founder of modern astronomy. He was born in Württemberg, Germany. While studying theology and mathematics at the University of Tübingen, he developed a strong conviction that God rules the universe by simple laws that can be described mathematically.

The chief aim of all investigations of the external world should be to discover the rational order and harmony which has been imposed on it by God and which He revealed to us in the language of mathematics.[20]

Since the time of Aristotle, astronomers had assumed that the planets follow circular orbits. Thus, Kepler was disturbed by an eight-minute difference between the observed orbit of Mars and that predicted by the circular model. He struggled with this discrepancy for years, convinced that planets must trace a geometric path.

Finally, Kepler realized that only an elliptical orbit would precisely explain the actual orbit. His landmark discovery led to his formulating the Three Laws of Planetary Motion, which revolutionized astronomy and physics. As a result, Kepler thereafter spoke of the eight-minute gap as a "gift of God."[21]

Kepler was one in a long line of monotheistic scientists who laid the foundation blocks for modern science. These trailblazers include: Francis Bacon (scientific method), Rene Descartes (analytic geometry), Isaac Newton (gravitation, optics, calculus), Blaise Pascal (probability studies and hydrostatics), Roger Boyle (chemistry), Michael Faraday (electromagnetism), John Mitchell (seismology), Gregor Mendel (genetics), Louis Pasteur (germ theory of disease), John Dalton (atomic theory), Bernhard Riemann (non-Euclidean geometry), James Simpson (anesthesiology), and James Joule (thermodynamics).[22]

Voltaire (1694 – 1788)

François Voltaire was born in Paris, and educated by Jesuits. He studied law, then turned to writing. At age twenty-three, he was imprisoned in the Bastille for lampooning the Duc d'Orleans. While in prison, though, he continued to write.

Voltaire's imprisonment, combined with his skeptical ideas, brought him international fame. Articulate and opinionated, he quickly became an influential enlightenment satirist, historian, and philosopher.

Voltaire was hostile to organized religion, especially Christianity. Nevertheless, he was convinced that God existed, and that the knowledge of God was innate:

> Among all peoples who use their reason there are universal opinions that seem imprinted by the master of our hearts. Such is the persuasion of the existence of God, and of his merciful justice . . .[23]

Voltaire believed the innate knowledge of God was confirmed by the intelligent design of the creation. "I shall always be convinced that a watch proves a watchmaker, and that a universe proves a God." Thus, he concluded, "to believe in a wise Creator, eternal and supreme, is not faith, it is reason."[24]

Edison (1847–1931)

Thomas Alva Edison is arguably America's greatest inventor. However, Edison attended school for only three months, while his family lived in Port Huron, Michigan. Thereafter, he was entirely self-taught.

At the age of twelve, while selling newspapers on the Grand Trunk Railway, Edison built a printing press in one of their freight cars. Using his press, Edison published a weekly newspaper, the Grand Trunk Herald.

This was the beginning of a lifetime of radical experimentation and innovation. Edison's inventions included the electric light, the phonograph, the motion picture camera, the electric storage battery, the mimeograph, and numerous other technological breakthroughs. Altogether, Edison patented over a thousand inventions.

Like other scientists, Edison benefited from the western confidence that God governs the universe by natural laws. He saw the reliability of those laws as proof for an infinitely intelligent Creator and Providence:

> I know this world is ruled by Infinite Intelligence. It required Infinite Intelligence to create it and it requires Infinite Intelligence to keep it on its course. Everything that surrounds us—everything that exists—proves that there are Infinite Laws behind it.

The complexity and order disclosed by science are further proof of a Supreme Intelligence. Thus, God's existence "could almost be proved from chemistry."[25]

Edison had a boundless confidence that God had a hidden technological solution for every problem. "I've been in the inventor business for thirty-three years," he told one man, "and my experience is that for every problem the Lord has made He has also made a solution."[26]

Hubble (1889–1953)

Edwin Hubble was born in Marshfield, Missouri. He studied mathematics and astronomy at Chicago University, then law at Oxford.

Hubble began to practice law at age 24, but he quickly left to make astronomy his career. In 1919, he began working at the Mount Wilson Observatory's new one-hundred-foot telescope—at the time, the largest in the world. Within five years, Hubble made the startling discovery that there are numerous galaxies outside our own Milky Way galaxy.

But Hubble's greatest discovery was yet to come. Most astronomers believed the universe was a relatively static place. However, in 1929, Hubble found that light from other galaxies is shifted to the red, meaning that they were moving away from the Milky Way. He then calculated that galaxies recede at a speed proportional to their distance from us. This relationship of distance to speed is now known as the Hubble Law, and it caused a revolution in the astronomical world. It demonstrated that the entire universe is expanding from a single, infinitely dense point.

Even religious skeptics now recognize the consistency between the Hubble Law and the Biblical account of creation. As noted by agnostic Robert Jastrow, founder of NASA's Goddard Institute, the Hubble Law "is one of the great discoveries in science: it is one of the main supports of the scientific story of Genesis."[27]

Hoyle (1915–2001)

Frederick Hoyle was born in West Yorkshire, England. He studied at Cambridge, where he then taught mathematics and became professor of astronomy. Hoyle also founded the world-renowned Institute of Theoretical Astronomy.

Hoyle's most important work has been on the origins of chemical elements. Scientists have frequently observed the difficulty in manufacturing all the elements necessary for life. Hoyle has demonstrated how particular elements are produced by fusion inside specific kinds of stars. For example, carbon can only be manufactured by an intricate process inside large stars.

Hoyle is a religious skeptic, so he has been baffled by the complexity of the processes necessary for the production of life-supporting elements. It is, he acknowledged, as if "the laws of nuclear physics have been deliberately designed with regard to the consequences they produce inside the stars."[28]

The universe, Hoyle says, looks like a "put-up job."[29] A common sense interpretation of the facts suggests that "a superintellect has monkeyed with physics, as well as with chemistry and biology," and that there are "no blind forces worth speaking about in nature." The probabilities one calculates "seem to me so overwhelming as to put this conclusion almost beyond question."[30]

Hawking (1942–)

Stephen William Hawking was born in Oxford, England. He studied at Oxford University, then has spent his career teaching at Cambridge. Since 1977, he has held the Cambridge Lucasian Chair for Mathematics, the same position held by Sir Isaac Newton.

Amazingly, since the 1960s, Hawking has been afflicted with a neuromotor disease, paralyzing most of his body. He is confined to a wheelchair, has lost his voice, and can communicate only by computer. Despite these daunting limitations, Hawking has been at the cutting edge of cosmology for over twenty years, researching such exotic subjects as black holes and the "Big Bang" origin of the universe.

Most people understand the Big Bang theory to mean that our three-dimensional universe exploded into existence about 15 billion years ago. However, Hawking has confirmed that our fourth dimension—time—*also* began in the Big Bang. In other words, before that point, time itself did not exist!

If that were not mind-boggling enough, Hawking notes that the Big Bang explosion had to occur with unbelievable precision for our universe to survive:

> If the rate of expansion one second after the big bang had been smaller by even one part in a hundred thousand million million, the universe would have recollapsed before it ever reached its present state.[31]

Hawking has also noted that the laws of physics contain many fixed "fundamental numbers," like the weight and charge of the electron.[32]

The remarkable fact is that the values of these numbers seem to have been very finely adjusted to make possible the development of life. For example, if the electric charge of the electron had been only slightly different, stars either would have been unable to burn hydrogen and helium, or else they would not have exploded.[33]

Thus, there are "relatively few ranges of values" for these numbers that would allow the development of "any form of intelligent life."[34] Most sets of values would give rise to universes that, "although they might be very beautiful, would contain no one able to wonder at that beauty."[35]

Scriptures

In our view, the Hebrew and Christian Scriptures teach monotheism with the greatest clarity. God existed before time began.[36] He created the universe out of nothing,[37] fine-tuned it for life,[38] and sustains it for his purposes.[39] He is all-powerful, and nothing can resist His will.[40]

God is all knowing and all wise.[41] He is beyond time, and sees the past, present and future with perfect clarity.[42] He governs the entire universe, yet He knows every individual. Every hair on our heads is numbered.[43]

As the Creator, Owner, and Ruler of the universe, God alone is worthy of worship. We should have no other gods before Him.[44] We should not deify any finite person, thing, or cause.[45]

Summary

From primitive religions to modern science, inquisitive people throughout history have concluded that the creation requires a Creator. He existed before time began. He designed and created matter and energy, and the laws that rule them.

However, we must not stop our analysis at this point. If there is an all-powerful God, then we should be concerned about our soul's fate. Do we measure up to God's moral standards? What are the consequences if we don't? The remainder of this book takes up these vital questions.

For further reading on Monotheism:

Barbour, Ian. *Religion and Science*. Harper San Francisco, 1997.
Cicero. *De Natura Deorum*.
Clark, Kelly, ed. *Philosophers Who Believe*. Intervarsity, 1993.
Dembski, William. *Intelligent Design*. Intervarsity, 1999.
Denton, Michael. *Nature's Destiny*. Free Press, 1998.
Glynn, Patrick. *God: The Evidence*. Forum, 1999.
Heeren, Fred. *Show Me God*. Searchlight, 1995.
Moreland, J.P., ed. *The Creation Hypothesis*. Intervarsity, 1994.
Pearcey, Nancy and Thaxton, Charles. *The Soul of Science*. Crossway, 1994.
Polkinghorne, John. *The Faith of a Physicist*. Princeton University Press, 1994.
Ross, Hugh. *The Creator and the Cosmos*. NavPress 3rd ed., 2001.
Schroeder, Gerald. *Genesis and the Big Bang*. Bantam, 1992.

2

The Moral Law: Do We Reap What We Sow?

SIDDHARTHA GAUTAMA was born in Nepal, India in 563 B.C.E., the son of a ruler of a small kingdom. He showed an early inclination to meditation and reflection that displeased his father, who wanted Siddhartha to be a soldier. To mollify his father, Siddhartha married at an early age and participated in the worldly life of the father's court. His life was sheltered, carefree, and boring.

At age twenty-nine, Siddhartha recognized the emptiness of his self-indulgent life. He saw that sickness and suffering were the common lot of humanity. Renouncing his family, wealth, and power, he embarked on a quest for truth. In particular, he sought a solution to universal human suffering.

For five years, Siddhartha followed the traditional Hindu practice of radical self-denial. However, he found that approach empty and unproductive.

Finally, Siddhartha had a flash of insight. Both sensual pleasure and self-denial are unprofitable. Instead, suffering is minimized by a balanced moral life. He called this life the "Middle Path," because it fell between the extremes of self-indulgence and self-denial.[46] It consisted of eight positive moral disciplines: right views, right intention, right speech, right action, right livelihood, right effort, right mindedness, and right contemplation.[47]

"Karma" guaranteed the effectiveness of this balanced moral life. Karma is universal justice, which gives actions eternal consequences. Good acts are rewarded with good consequences. Bad acts are punished with bad consequences. When an action ripens, one experiences the fruits of this action, "be it in this life, or be it in the next life, or be it in any other future life."[48] Thus, good acts reduce suffering in this life and the next.

Once Siddhartha was converted to this pursuit of morality, he quickly attracted a large group of disciples. For the next forty-five years he traveled, taught, and established monastic communities.

After Siddhartha's death, his followers continued to multiply. His Middle Path filled a great void in Indian culture, defining a practical morality that reduced suffering for the common person. His grateful disciples gave Siddhartha a special title—the "Enlightened One" or the "Buddha."

Siddhartha's conviction about moral consequences is not an isolated one. A study of the world's literature discloses a widespread belief in a universal moral law. This law judges the morality of all human conduct, rewarding the good and punishing the bad. The rewards and punishments begin in this life, and are completed in the next.

Egyptian Book of the Dead (c. 1600 B.C.E.)

Virtually all world religions believe that the soul survives death and then enters a state of reward or punishment. This belief is evident in one of the earliest surviving Egyptian inscriptions, dating back to 3600 B.C.E., the dawn of recorded history. The inscription provided guidance to a dying person, to prevent his heart from "falling away from him into the underworld."[49] The person's fate would be decided in a "hearing," where his words would be weighed in "the Balance."[50]

A text from 2500 B.C.E. clarified that the dead are judged by moral criteria. The person is condemned if "he has done deeds against that which is very right and true."[51]

Finally, around 1600 B.C.E., the time-tested Egyptian texts were gathered into a single scroll, the *Book of the Dead*. In this document, Egyptians learned what to expect in the next life. They would face a panel of judges, who would question them about specific moral breaches. They would have to defend their earthly conduct. The "feather of truth" was near their lips, and would judge the accuracy of their words.

To avoid eternal punishment, each person would have to prove that he had led a life free from specific acts of immorality:

> I have done no wrong . . . I have not robbed . . . I have not murdered . . . I have not told lies . . . I have not trespassed . . . I have not gossiped . . . I have not committed adultery . . . I have not made myself deaf to the words of right and truth . . . I have not judged hastily.[52]

Only the person who passed this rigorous test would be admitted into eternal life. The remainder would be condemned to punishment in the underworld.

Zoroaster (630–550 B.C.E.)

Zoroaster was born in the Persian land of Airyana Vaejah. His homeland was mountainous, and its people were devoted to the raising of cattle. While still a young man, Zoroaster began teaching that there is one God, the Creator, who will reward good and punish evil in the next life.

Initially, Zoroaster's teachings were strongly resisted by priests of the traditional Persian religions. However, he eventually gained the support of Vishtaspa, the king of Chorasmia, which is now Turkistan. With the king's help, Zoroaster's doctrines became widely known and accepted.

Zoroaster believed that people have a free will. He taught that every person faces a moral conflict in this life—a battle between good and evil. However, in the next life, there will be no such conflict. God has total domination, and will punish all evil thoughts, words, and deeds.

Zoroaster taught that, after a person dies, the soul faces judgment on the "Bridge of the Requiter." There, the person's good and evil deeds flash before his eyes. Those whose "thoughts and words, deeds and religion are good" can cross the Bridge and enter the kingdom of everlasting joy and light.[53] However, those whose deeds are evil are dragged off the Bridge into "nethermost hell," a region of punishment and darkness.[54]

Confucius (551–479 B.C.E.)

Confucius is one of the most influential figures in Chinese history. However, his life began inauspiciously. He was born in the state of Lu, the present-day province of Shantung. Feudalism had degenerated in China, and crime and corruption were rampant. Confucius' father died three years after he was born, leaving the family in poverty.

Confucius did menial work until the age of twenty-three, when his mother died. With family ties severed, he began his career as a teacher, traveling about China and instructing a small group of disciples. He taught the ancient Chinese classics, focusing on the benefits of morality.

Confucius believed that moral leaders were the key to a prosperous society. If rulers would live virtuous lives, they would influence the common people by the power of example. As a result, their states would become prosperous and happy.

Confucius taught the need to harmonize life with the moral law. The life of the moral man is "an exemplification of the universal moral order."[55] On the other hand, the "vulgar person's life" is a "contradiction of the universal moral order," because in his heart he has "no regard for, or fear of, the moral law."[56]

Confucius believed that a moral law implied a Moral Lawgiver. To show "respect for the moral law" is to "understand the law of God."[57]

Confucius recognized that the core principle of the moral law is unselfishness—avoiding harm to others. When one carries out the principles of "conscientiousness and reciprocity," he is close to the moral law. "What you do not wish others should do unto you, do not do unto others."[58]

At the age of fifty, Confucius was given the chance to put his theories to the test. He was appointed minister of crime in the state of Lu, and his administration was remarkably successful. For fifteen years, he reformed the criminal justice system. He enforced the laws in an even-handed way, and crime was virtually eliminated.

However, Confucius' success was his downfall as a leader. The reduction of crime made Lu such a powerful state that it aroused the jealousy of a neighboring prince, who maneuvered to have Confucius removed as minister.

Confucius dedicated the remainder of his life to teaching and writing on the classics. Following his death, his disciples gathered his teachings and writings into the Four Books (Shi Shu) of Confucian literature. These became the standard textbooks for succeeding Chinese generations.

Aeschylus (525–456 B.C.E.)

Aeschylus was born in Eleusis, near Athens. He quickly proved to be a brilliant dramatist and poet. At age twenty-five he produced his first play—the first of ninety. He was the first great tragic poet in Athens, and is often called the father of Greek tragedy.

Aeschylus was an innovator. Traditional Greek plays were limited to a single actor, often playing multiple roles. He introduced a second actor, creating many possibilities for dramatic dialogue.

Aeschylus used his plays to teach moral retribution. For example, in *Agamemnon*, a faithless wife murders her husband

(King Agamemnon) when he returns home from war. Their son avenges the father, murdering the mother. Finally, heaven punishes the son. The moral of the play: an eternal law of moral retribution. "The spoiler is robbed; he has killed, he has paid. The truth stands ever beside God's throne eternal: he who has wrought shall pay; that is law."[59]

Motse (468–401 B.C.E.)

Motse was born in China after the death of Confucius, when the centralized Chou Dynasty was disintegrating, and China was dividing into small, warring feudal states. Growing up in this climate of uncertainty, he developed a lifelong desire to bring political and social order out of chaos.

Motse became a strong advocate of rational thinking and methodology in all aspects of life, especially in government. Contradicting Chinese traditions, he taught that government advancement should be based upon merit, not age or social status. Leaders should test, measure, and apply standards that achieve demonstrable results that benefit all classes of people.

Motse spent most of his life traveling from one feudal state to another, searching for princes who would institute his teachings. He also maintained a school and trained his disciples for administrative positions. His teachings had impact on Chinese thought for centuries.

Motse's belief in the rational life was fueled in part by his belief that heaven ruled the world, rewarding moral behavior and punishing evil behavior. It is in a person's self-interest to avoid immoral behavior. "When man does not do what Heaven desires, but what Heaven abominates, Heaven will also not do what man desires, but what he abominates."[60]

The long-term consequences of moral choices show that heaven prefers virtue to wickedness. With righteousness the world becomes "rich" and "orderly." Without righteousness, the world becomes "poor" and "chaotic."[61]

The punishment of evil conduct shows heaven's concern for humanity. For the murder of one innocent individual, for example, there will be one calamity. "Who is it that sends down the calamity? It is Heaven." If heaven did not love people, there would be no such retribution.[62]

Socrates (470–399 B.C.E.)

Socrates was born in Athens, Greece, the son of a sculptor and a midwife. After receiving the traditional education in literature and music, he taught himself philosophy.

Initially, Socrates pursued his father's trade, producing some noteworthy statues for Athens. Then, in his late thirties and early forties, he fought with distinction as a soldier in the Peloponnesian War with Sparta. This war had great symbolic value for ancient Greece, pitting the intellectual Athenians against the militaristic Spartans.

Following the war, Socrates believed he received a divine command to avoid politics and pursue philosophy. He devoted himself full-time to teaching, encouraging Athenians to engage in moral self-examination and tend to their souls.

Socrates taught the objective reality of moral principles such as justice, virtue, and love. Through Plato and other disciples, Socrates forever changed the course of western philosophy.

However, Socrates' teachings were not well received by the establishment of his day. Many Athenian leaders disliked his attitude towards the state and religion. In 399 B.C.E., he was charged with neglecting the Greek gods, and was sentenced to death.

Socrates' disciples planned his escape from prison, but he preferred to comply with the law and die for his cause. He consoled his disciples that the real Socrates consisted not of his mortal body, but of his immortal soul.[63]

Since every soul survives death, Socrates taught, its fate in the next world depends on how one has behaved in this world. Justice requires such a universal judgment:

> If death were a release from everything, it would be a boon for the wicked, because by dying they would be released not only from the body, but also from their own wickedness together with the soul.[64]

This doctrine of future punishment promotes "self-control, and goodness, and courage, and liberality, and truth" in this life.[65]

Cicero (106–43 B.C.E.)

Marcus Tullius Cicero was born into a wealthy family in Arpinu, in modern-day Italy. After receiving an excellent education in Greece, he served in the Roman military under the noted general Pompeius Strabo, the father of Pompey.

In his mid-twenties, Cicero began a brilliant legal career in the Roman courts. He proved to be a dazzling advocate and orator, successfully representing many prominent citizens.

At age thirty-one, Cicero entered government service in Sicily as a *quaestor*—a financial administrator. Nine years later he was appointed a *praetor*, a judicial officer of great power. At age forty-three he was elected consul to the Roman Senate.

Cicero wrote several important philosophical and political treatises, and made many significant speeches in the Senate. Through these, he tried to uphold republican principles during the civil wars that destroyed the Roman Republic and led to Julius Caesar's dictatorship.

Cicero's central thesis was that a single moral law governs all people. It is "unchanging and eternal." Its prohibitions deter people from wrongdoing. Its commands "call people to their duty."[66]

Accordingly, Cicero taught, human laws couldn't modify this universal law. "We cannot be exempted from this law by any decree of the Senate or the people."[67]

Behind this universal law is the universal lawgiver. God is its author, promulgator, and enforcer. He is the "lord and master of us all."[68]

Such views obviously could not be reconciled with Caesar's dictatorship. Moreover, Cicero's candor and piercing oratory had made many powerful enemies, including Caesar's adopted son Octavian. On December 7, 43 B.C.E., Octavian had Cicero executed.

Epictetus (50–120 C.E.)

Epictetus was born a Roman slave in Hierapolis, in modern-day Turkey. As a youth, while still a slave, he studied the Greek philosophy of Stoicism.

After his master granted him freedom, Epictetus became an influential philosopher. He taught in Rome until the age of thirty-five, when Emperor Domitian exiled Epictetus and several other Stoic philosophers. Nevertheless, Epictetus continued his discourses, which were transcribed by his student Arrian, who was later to achieve renown as a Greek historian.

Foundational to Epictetus' worldview was the existence and oversight of God. "[We must] first learn that there is a God, and that His Providence directs the Universe; further, that to hide from Him not only one's acts but even one's thoughts and intentions is impossible."[69]

A person should live knowing that "every single act of his was under the eye of God."[70] We should not live "under the wrath of God, but be obedient unto Him."[71]

Ignoring God's judgment has adverse consequences in life. "As God has ordained, so do; otherwise you will suffer chastisement and loss."[72]

Rather than being concerned with the opinions and laws of the day, a person should seek what is good and in accordance with reason. "These are the Laws ordained of God—these are His Edicts; these a man should expound and interpret, to these submit himself, not the laws of [men]."[73] Neglect of God's laws leads only to "failure, ill success . . . and hindrance."[74]

Epictetus' teachings brought him a mixture of success and adversity. However, after his death, they had a tremendous impact. His doctrines were eagerly absorbed by the next generation, including Roman emperor Marcus Aurelius. And they continue to be read throughout the world today.

Hume (1711–1776)

David Hume is perhaps the greatest of all British philosophers. Sir Isaiah Berlin wrote of Hume: "No man has influenced the history of philosophy to a deeper and more disturbing degree."[75]

At the age of twelve, Hume enrolled in Scotland's Edinburgh University, where he developed a lifelong love for philosophy. Influenced by the rigorous logic of scientist Isaac Newton, Hume sought to apply the same empirical methods to moral and religious subjects.

In religion, Hume became a skeptic. He did not find the traditional arguments for God's existence to be convincing. However, in morals, Hume came to a different conclusion. He became an advocate for a naturalistic moral system.

First, Hume noted the importance society attached to moral conduct. Morality is "a subject that interests us above all others."[76] Our passion is engaged because people believe the "peace of society" is at stake when morals are at risk.[77]

Indeed, moral ideas hold a powerful influence over individual decisions. Common experience informs us that people "are often governed by their duties."[78] That is, people are commonly deterred from some actions "by the opinion of injustice," and impelled to other actions by a sense of "obligation."[79]

These moral distinctions are derived from an inner moral impulse, an emotional sense of right and wrong. Virtue gives us a feeling of "satisfaction." Vice gives us a feeling of "uneasiness."[80]

These moral sentiments are "so rooted in our constitution and temper" that, absent disease or madness, it is "impossible to extirpate and destroy them."[81]

Hume recognized that morality is determined by motives, not by outward conduct. A mere external performance has no merit. Actions simply serve as external signs of the motives that produced them.[82]

Kant (1724–1804)

Immanuel Kant was born in Konigsberg, Prussia, in modern-day Russia. He received a classical education at the Fredericianum College, then obtained a doctorate in physics and mathematics at the University of Konigsberg.

Kant taught at the University for forty-two years, starting in science and mathematics, then gradually enlarging his field of expertise to cover virtually all branches of philosophy. He sought to uncover the laws of the universe as revealed by reason alone.

Kant's original thinking attracted numerous students, but his rationalistic religious views brought him into conflict with the Prussian government. Ultimately, in 1792, when Kant was 68 years old, King Frederick William II forbade him to teach or write on religious subjects.

Kant was not an orthodox Christian. However, he believed that both nature and the conscience provide evidence for a Creator. The person who wishes answers to life's ultimate questions must contemplate not only "the starry heavens above" but also "the moral law within."[83]

The conscience is irrational if it does not point to an independent law. Kant likened its operations to a criminal trial, in which the person's guilt or innocence is determined by an impartial judge. If the conscience were a mere extension of the person, it would always justify the individual. The fact that we do not always win such a trial demonstrates that the conscience represents an objective standard, beyond mere self-justification.[84]

Kant was skeptical that any human action, no matter how noble, could be motivated purely by moral duty. Most moral acts can be traced to a "refined self-love."[85] Even the closest self-examination may not disclose the selfish motive. Yet, even if we cannot identify the specific selfish motive, we cannot from this infer with certainty that it was not really some "secret impulse from self-love."[86]

Kant concluded that only the sense of accountability to the Creator could keep people moral. Because people who see only outward conduct enforce human laws, they cannot regulate the heart, which is the seat of morality. There must therefore be someone other than the populace who can be the lawgiver in a moral community.[87] He must be "one who knows the heart" in order to see into "the innermost parts of the disposition of each individual."[88] Therefore, a happy society will honor God as the "moral ruler of the world."[89]

Washington (1732–1799)

George Washington is well-known for his public accomplishments. He led the American forces during the Revolutionary War, refused to be America's first king, presided over the Constitutional Convention, and served as the nation's first president. Most historians believe he was essential to America's survival as a republic.

However, his public achievements were extensions of the inner man. Washington had a distinct philosophy of life. He believed that God rules the world in justice. Thus, he constantly emphasized the vital connection between prosperity and moral virtue.

For instance, when the British were forced to retreat from Boston during the Revolution, Washington saw it as God's merciful intervention based on the justice of the American position. Addressing the Massachusetts legislature, he noted that the colony was now relieved from the cruel and oppressive invasions of those who sought to "erect the standard of lawless domination, and to trample on the rights of humanity." The fact that this victory was accomplished without the shedding of blood "must be ascribed to the interposition of that Providence, which has manifestly appeared in our behalf through the whole of this important struggle."[90]

Likewise, when the French intervened in the war to help the Americans, Washington proclaimed a day of thanksgiving for the troops:

> It having pleased the Almighty Ruler of the Universe propitiously to defend the Cause of the United American States and finally by raising us up a powerful Friend among the Princes of the Earth to establish our liberty and independence upon lasting foundations, it becomes us to set apart a day for gratefully acknowledging the divine Goodness and celebrating the important Event which we owe to his benign Interposition.[91]

Recognizing human corruption, Washington knew that the country could not truly merit God's intervention. Instead, he saw the justice of the cause as a necessary condition for providential aid. As a result, success in the Revolution placed the nation under a debt to God: "The hand of Providence has been so conspicuous in all this that he must be worse than an infidel that lacks faith, and more than wicked that has not gratitude to acknowledge his obligations."[92]

Washington did not forget this lesson. Following the War, he constantly spoke of the connection between virtue and prosperity. In his first inaugural address he told the nation:

> [T]here is no truth more thoroughly established, than that there exists in the economy and course of nature, an indis-

> soluble union between virtue and happiness, between duty and advantage, between the genuine maxims of an honest and magnanimous policy, and the solid rewards of public prosperity and felicity.[93]

Thus, "the propitious smiles of Heaven" cannot be expected by a nation that disregards "the eternal rules of order and right, which Heaven itself has ordained."[94]

Washington frequently showed mixed feelings about fame and public applause. He recognized that virtue is more important than popularity. Writing to his friend Henry Lee, Washington noted that he prized the "good opinion of my fellow citizens." However, "if I know myself, I would not seek or retain popularity at the expense of one social duty or moral virtue."[95]

Washington's strong conviction about God's moral rule was tempered by an awareness of human suffering, which often seemed unjust. For example, on one occasion, tragedy simultaneously struck the households of Washington and a family friend, Burwell Bassett, when both families lost a daughter. Washington wrote Bassett a letter of consolation. "[T]he ways of Providence [are] inscrutable, and the justice of it [is] not to be scanned by the shallow eye of humanity."[96]

Schiller (1759–1805)

Johann Christoph Friedrich von Schiller was born in Württemberg, Germany, the son of the estate manager for the Duke of Württemberg. After being educated at the Duke's military school, he studied law and medicine. At the age of twenty-one, he was appointed physician to a military regiment stationed in Stuttgart.

Schiller made considerable sacrifices, though, to pursue his work as a writer and dramatist. When he was twenty-three, his first play, *The Robbers*, was presented at the National Theater in Mannheim. However, when Schiller left Württemberg to witness the play's production, the Duke had him imprisoned for leaving the city without permission, and prohibited him from publishing further dramatic works.

Schiller escaped from prison. During the next ten years, he lived in various parts of Germany. He continued his writing, usually under an assumed name to avoid extradition to Württemberg. Eventually he settled in Weimar, where he completed several historical dramas, including his most widely known, *William Tell*.

Schiller is now recognized as the greatest dramatist in the history of German theater. His works had great emotional power, and he used the stage to illustrate issues of morality and justice.

Schiller had experienced injustice and suffering first hand. Nevertheless, he saw God closely monitoring human history, to judge all immorality. "The history of the world is its judgment."[97]

Schiller's belief in moral retribution was not limited to "big picture" issues such as the rise and fall of nations. The same principle applied to individuals. Our current circumstances represent God's judgment on the immoral conduct we and others have previously done. "For every event is a judgment from God."[98]

Lincoln (1809–1865)

Abraham Lincoln is considered by many historians to be America's greatest president. Scholars who study the Civil War are amazed that he was able to maintain northern support for the war, given the brutal losses the federal army suffered in almost every battle.

Obviously Lincoln was a very intelligent man with exceptional diplomatic skills. But was there something more? Did he have a special mindset that took him through the bitter setbacks, giving him confidence that the north would ultimately prevail?

Near the beginning of the Civil War, Lincoln gave an address to Congress on saving the Union. God would judge the nation as a whole, he said, by how it treated the slave. "In giving freedom to the slave, we assure freedom to the free."[99]

Therefore, Lincoln concluded, the best way to save the Union was to free the slaves. It was a risky but honorable strategy. "We shall nobly save, or meanly lose, the last best, hope of earth."[100]

Though God's ways are often mysterious, Lincoln believed they were just. "He has destroyed nations from the map of history for their sins."[101]

However, Lincoln told friends, God's way of accomplishing the end of slavery "may be different from theirs."[102] It might be God's will to extend the war. If so, the suffering was for the good—for "the great ends He ordains."[103] "Surely He intends some great good to follow this mighty convulsion, which no mortal could make, and no mortal could stay."[104]

Lincoln was concerned that God might extend the Civil War as punishment for the nation's immorality. Thus, in 1863, he issued a proclamation appointing a national fast day. The proclamation recognized the "just Government of Almighty God in all the affairs of men and of nations." He also raised a vital question about God's justice and the Civil War:

> [I]nasmuch as we know that, by His divine law, nations like individuals are subjected to punishments and chastisement in this world, may we not justly fear that the awful calamity of civil war which now desolates the land may be but a punishment inflicted upon us for our presumptuous sins to the needful end of our national reformation as a whole people.[105]

In his second inaugural address, during the final year of the Civil War, Lincoln suggested that the conflict was God's punishment on the nation for tolerating the cruel institution of slavery:

> Fondly do we hope—fervently do we pray—that this mighty scourge of war may speedily pass away. Yet, if God wills that it continue, until all the wealth piled by the bondman's two hundred and fifty years of unrequited toil shall be sunk, and until every drop of blood drawn with the lash, shall be paid by another drawn with the sword, as was said three thousand years ago, so still it must be said "the judgments of the Lord are true and righteous altogether."[106]

Kagan (1929–)

Jerome Kagan is Professor of Developmental Psychology at Harvard University. He is famous for his pioneering work in the study of infancy and cognitive development.

Kagan's research blends psychology with intellectual history, anthropology, and philosophy. His synthesis has challenged many of psychology's most deeply held assumptions—arguing, for example, that early experience does not inexorably shape our lives and that the family's influence is more subtle than previously supposed.

Kagan has also challenged the assumption that morality is merely a social norm, imposed by society. His research has disclosed how quickly and naturally children develop a moral sense. An appreciation of moral standards emerges early in development, "long before language and motor coordination."[107] By the age of three, children become concerned about "standards on prohibited behavior."[108]

For example, three-year-olds from very different cultures show obvious signs of anxiety or shame when they fail an adult's request to build a tower of blocks. Such observations suggest that "an appreciation of good or bad is a universal . . . competence that emerges early in development, like laughter or fear of strangers."[109]

Thus, children are in a sense "programmed" to commit themselves to an "ethical mission."[110] Humans are "driven to invent moral criteria" as "newly hatched turtles move toward water and moths toward light."[111]

Without this fundamental moral sense, a child "could not be socialized."[112] All children must, because they are human, realize that causing hurt to another is immoral. "Such knowledge can never be lost, regardless of any subsequent cruelty the child may have experienced."[113]

People are constantly insisting that one outcome is "more virtuous than others."[114] Thus, the "ideas of good and bad" will "always be a critical human concern."[115]

Scriptures

In our view, the Hebrew and Christian Scriptures describe the moral law with the greatest consistency and clarity. The root moral principle is love—love for God and love for people. All the particular moral commands depend upon these.[116]

However, this love is not a subjective sentimentality. It has content. It has external, objective criteria. These are, in summary form: (1) no other gods, (2) no idols, (3) no profanity, (4) keep the Sabbath, (5) honor parents, (6) no murder, (7) no adultery, (8) no stealing, (9) no perjury, and (10) no coveting.[117]

By evaluating our behavior in light of these ten commandments, we can determine whether we are truly loving God and people, or whether we are just deluding ourselves into thinking we are "good people."

At first glance, many of the Ten Commandments seem possible to keep. Most of us do not physically murder, steal, or commit adultery. However, the Scriptures state that the commands apply to internal motives, not just to external acts. If I hate other people, I have murdered them in my heart.[118] If I lust, I have committed adultery in my heart.[119]

By that standard, we violate the Commandments every day. By our selfish motives, we violate the moral law, even if the resulting outward acts appear good. That is why Jesus so strongly condemned hypocrisy—i.e., pretending to be good when our inner self is bad.[120] When we are hypocrites, we are like whitewashed tombs—outwardly beautiful but inwardly full of death and corruption.[121]

Our motives—what is in our heart—are the real person.[122] God looks at our motives, not our outwardly good works.[123] Even if we fool ourselves, God is not fooled. "All a man's ways seem right to him, but God weighs the heart."[124]

Therefore, to be a good person, we must have unselfish motives. We must love God and people. We must keep the Ten Commandments, both with our external behavior and with our inward motives.

What are the consequences of violating the moral law? According to the Scriptures, there are consequences in this life. God has built the universe on moral foundations. There is a moral order—a system of moral cause and effect. In the long run, we reap what we sow.[125] We enjoy the "fruit" of good acts.[126] We are "ensnared" by the results of bad acts.[127]

However, these good or bad consequences are not the end of the story. They are only natural consequences, in this life. These natural consequences are incomplete, as all who see injustice in the world can attest. Bad people are seldom fully punished. Evildoers often seem to prosper, and are not fully held to account.[128]

The judgment in the next life corrects all such imbalances. According to the Scriptures, God will judge all thoughts, motives, words, and deeds.[129] All immoral acts will be fully punished. No bad acts will be forgotten. The judgment will be accurate and impartial. Complete justice will be done.[130]

Summary

The moral law is both comforting and disturbing. Comforting, because the injustices in this life will be corrected. No evildoer will escape. All people will receive impartial, permanent justice.

However, the moral law is also disturbing. The standard seems impossibly high. Can any of our acts be truly unselfish? In the next chapter, we will consider whether any person can satisfy the strict demands of the moral law.

For further reading on the moral law:

Aquinas, Thomas. *Summa Theologica*. Questions 90-97.
Brandon, S.G.F. *The Judgment of the Dead*. Scribner's, 1967.
Coward, Harold. Life After Death in World Religions. Orbis, 1997.
Fuchs, Josef. *Natural Law*. Sheed & Ward, 1965.
Green, Ronald M. *Religion and Moral Reason*. Oxford, 1988.
Kevan, Ernest. *Moral Law*. P & R Publishing, 1991.
Kreeft, Peter. *Back to Virtue*. Ignatius, 1992.
Lewis, C.S. *The Abolition of Man*. Macmillan, 1947.
Lippmann, Walter. A *Preface to Morals*. Macmillan, 1929.
Plato. *Laws*.
Plutarch. *On the Delays of the Divine Vengeance*.

3

Human Nature: Are We Bad to the Bone?

ERNEST BECKER spent his childhood in the pleasant and tranquil city of Springfield, Massachusetts. He went on to distinction as a decorated American soldier in World War II. However, near the end of the war, he and his command liberated a Nazi concentration camp. Becker then faced firsthand the depths of cruelty that were possible even in "civilized" Europe.

Becker could not forget his experience. After receiving a doctorate in anthropology, he began to write extensively on the problem of human evil. At first, he started with the assumption that human nature is good, and that evil is the product of the community's repression of individual freedom. Evil results when the individual is alienated by "large impersonal forces beyond his control."[131]

The solution was a rational, top-down approach, where society provided individuals with more choices and freedom.[132] This would strengthen self-esteem, which is the "surest basis for true selflessness and social harmony."[133]

However, by the time Becker published his final book in 1975, *Escape from Evil*, his analysis had undergone a complete transformation. He no longer located the source of evil in repressive social institutions. Instead, Becker concluded, the problem was within the human heart. All people are motivated by an instinct for self-preservation that causes us to lash out at others. This was the key to explaining the vicious nature of human behavior. Becker believed he was finally looking "man in the face for the first time in my career."[134]

Becker's conclusion is disturbing, but he is not alone. Every generation sees fresh evidence of human depravity. Throughout history, many careful thinkers have concluded that the human heart is defective. Selfishness seems to stain even the most enlightened conduct.

Plato (428–348 B.C.E.)

Plato was born into an aristocratic family in the prosperous city of Athens, Greece. A disciple of Socrates, Plato founded the Academy, the first European university, which continued in operation for over 900 years. At the Academy, Plato taught many young philosophers, including his most famous pupil, Aristotle. In turn, Aristotle was the instructor of Alexander the Great, the Macedonian king who conquered the Persian Empire and spread Greek ideals throughout the world.

In addition to being a link in such an important chain, Plato was perhaps the most brilliant of the ancient Greek philosophers. He synthesized Greek thought around the central theme of virtue. He also formulated, in *The Republic*, a description of an ideal state.

Despite his apparently idealistic framework, though, Plato did not romanticize human behavior. Instead, he recognized that every person is guilty of the ultimate moral failing—excessive "love of self."[135] This is the gravest of all faults.[136] It is the source of our misdeeds. It is "inborn" in the souls of men.[137]

This offense is inherently self-indulgent. The eye of love is blind where "the beloved," self, is concerned. And so a person proves a bad judge of right, good, and honor in his own life, expecting more praise than he deserves.[138]

Plato also recognized that self-love can never ultimately be eradicated. In all of us, even in good people, there is "a terrible, fierce, and lawless brood of desires."[139] Instead, the best we can do is to recognize the wisdom and benefits of virtue, and live morally based upon self-interest. The temperate, courageous, and wise person has more pleasure and less pain than the cowardly, foolish, and licentious person.[140] Thus, the person who has virtue is "absolutely and unreservedly happier" than the person who lives in depravity.[141]

Hsun Tzu (312–238 B.C.E.)

Hsun Tzu is a major figure in Chinese philosophy. Along with Confucius and Mencius, he is one of the great founders of Confucianism. He was the first Confucian to produce a book rather than leaving sayings for later compilation, and his writing brought a new intellectual rigor to Confucian debate.

Hsun Tzu grew up in Chao in northern China. At the age of fifty, he traveled to Ch'i, the city where the leading Chinese scholars congregated. He was quickly recognized as their most eminent philosopher, and achieved renown for his trailblazing work in psychology, law, and logic. He also challenged the assumption of many Chinese philosophers that human nature is essentially good.

Those who champion the goodness of humanity do not know "the nature of man."[142] In other words, they do not understand "the distinction between man's nature and his effort."[143]

Hsun Tzu concluded "the nature of man is evil." Our "inborn nature is to seek for gain" and to be "envious and hate others." To follow this nature "will inevitably result in strife and rapacity, combine with rebellion and disorder, and end in violence."[144]

Hsun Tzu taught that this defect in human nature could be corrected by the "civilizing influence of teachers and laws."[145] However, he did not explain how goodness could be expected from teachers and lawgivers, who themselves have evil natures.

Seneca (4 B.C.E.–65 C.E.)

Lucius Seneca was born in Cordoba, Spain, the son of renowned Roman orator Marcus Seneca. Lucius Seneca received a thorough education in rhetoric and philosophy in Rome, where he became a champion of Stoic philosophy. He developed exceptional skills as a dramatist and writer, and is today considered one of the leading figures in Latin literature.

In 49 C.E., Seneca was appointed tutor to Nero, who became emperor in the year 54 C.E. Much of the decency and moderation of Nero's early rule is attributed to the rational guidance of Seneca. By 62 C.E., however, Seneca had lost all influence with the emperor, who quickly degenerated into a sadist and a tyrant. Nero sought to confiscate Seneca's family wealth, and attempted to have Seneca poisoned. In 65 C.E., there was an unsuccessful attempt to kill Nero, and Seneca had a connection to the assassins. This was all the excuse Nero needed. Seneca was immediately condemned, and he committed suicide by imperial order.

Seneca saw great cruelty in his life, but he did not put the blame on "a few bad apples." Instead, he had a realistic view of the human heart. No sensible person will hate wrongdoers—"otherwise he will hate himself." A person having difficulty with this concept should reflect, "How many times he offends against morality, how many of his acts stand in need of pardon." No one is found who can "acquit himself."[146] We are all wicked; "each man will find in his own breast the fault which he censures in another."[147]

Thus, Seneca concluded, humanity needs divine moral help. "[T]here is no good man without God."[148] No one has strength of himself to emerge from wickedness—"someone must hold forth a hand; someone must draw us out."[149]

Plutarch (46–125 C.E.)

Plutarch was born in Greece, and educated in Athens. After traveling widely in the Roman Empire, he lectured in Rome on moral philosophy. He was a popular teacher, and was known by his students as a genial guide and philosopher.

Plutarch wrote numerous biographies, including *Parallel Lives of Illustrious Greeks and Romans*, which compared the lives of famous historical figures. Shakespeare closely followed Plutarch's lives when composing his plays on Roman history, including *Julius Caesar* and *Antony and Cleopatra.*

Plutarch's books portrayed character and its moral implications. Character development, he wrote, starts with an accurate assessment of the challenge. We have a mental handicap, causing us to reach for too much. "The culprit is self-love, which impels men to crave primacy and victory in everything."[150] All human nature bears its crop of "contention, jealousy and envy."[151] In fact, he concluded, it is impossible to find "any deed that is faultless as regards its virtue."[152]

La Rochefoucauld (1613–1680 C.E.)

Francois duc de La Rochefoucauld was born to a wealthy French family, and in many ways had an ideal life. He was the heir of a great noble house, married a wealthy heiress, and had a large and affectionate family. He succeeded to his father's dukedom, and was highly influential in the court of King Louis XIII.

By middle age, though, the glamour of wealth and power had lost much of its luster for Rochefoucauld. He reflected on society, and the motives underlying virtuous acts. Finally, at the age of fifty-two, he published his *Maxims*, with page after page of pithy observations about human conduct. The book was an instant success, and is credited with forever changing French culture, giving it a clarity and realism about human motivation. It was, as historian Leonard Tancock has recently noted, "perhaps the most penetrating and disconcerting" book ever written about human nature.[153]

Rochefoucauld analyzed a variety of selfish motives for good behavior. Virtue often arises from our "wish to deserve the praise of others."[154] Empathy towards the less fortunate is usually an extension of our own fears for the future, a way of preparing ourselves emotionally—a "precaution against misfortunes that may befall us."[155] Likewise, the love of justice is generally the "fear of suffering injustice."[156] Repentance is "not so much regret for the evil we have done" as "fear of the evil that may befall us as a result."[157]

Thus, Rochefoucauld acknowledged, good deeds are an intelligent and far-sighted way of securing our own happiness. Self-interest "sets in motion virtues . . . of all kinds."[158] However, we then delude ourselves by pretending that our motives are truly altruistic. "Self-interest speaks all manner of tongues and plays all manner of parts, even that of disinterestedness."[159] We can easily fool ourselves about our motives, since "the head is always fooled by the heart."[160] But it is more difficult to persuade those who know us. It is as easy to "deceive ourselves without noticing" as it is "hard to deceive others without their noticing."[161]

Franklin (1706–1790)

Benjamin Franklin epitomizes the American ideal of the "self-made man." Starting from near poverty, he earned a fortune in publishing and other ventures. Though lacking formal education, he taught himself so well that he became a world-renowned scientist for his discoveries in electricity.

Franklin developed radical views on a number of subjects. In politics, he supported the American Revolution before it was popular. In religion he was a Deist, believing in a distant Creator who seldom interfered in human affairs.

Franklin sought to apply his optimistic, can-do spirit to moral development. First, he compiled a list of thirteen virtues: temperance, silence, order, resolution, frugality, industry, sincerity, justice, moderation, cleanliness, tranquillity, chastity, and humility. Next he kept a daily log, recording his progress in each virtue. At first he found numerous faults. But, over time, "I had the satisfaction of seeing them diminish."[162]

Eventually, Franklin was satisfied that he had developed most of the virtues. Unfortunately, he was unable to make much progress in the last one on the list—humility. Thus, he decided, he would have to be satisfied with the "appearance" of humility.[163]

Similarly, Franklin never got beyond the motive of self-interest. In fact, his entire system for developing virtue was based upon enlightened self-interest. The virtues were desirable because of their long-term benefits. They were in "everyone's interest, who wish'd to be happy."[164]

Blackstone (1723–1780)

William Blackstone entered Oxford University at age fifteen. After graduating, he began training for a legal career. Organized legal schooling in England was largely nonexistent in that day, and there were no systematic books explaining the law. Thus, like other aspiring attorneys, he had to learn "on the job" and by using antiquated and narrowly-focused legal texts.

At age twenty, while practicing as an attorney, Blackstone began teaching undergraduate law at Oxford. His course was immensely popular, and it became the basis for his renowned *Commentaries on the Laws of England*. The *Commentaries* provided, for the first time, a systematic overview of English law. Clearly and elegantly written, they were accessible to lawyers, students, and business people. They had a powerful impact in both England and the American colonies, and were heavily utilized through the end of the nineteenth century.

Blackstone's *Commentaries* were successful, in part, because they explained the rationale for human laws. He showed how they were an outgrowth of both the moral law and human self-interest. God has "enabled human reason to discover" the "eternal, immutable laws of good and evil" so far as they are necessary for the "conduct of human actions."[165]

God, in his goodness, has made it in the interest of humanity to discover these basic moral principles. He has "inseparably interwoven the laws of eternal justice with the happiness of each individual," so that happiness cannot be attained without observing justice.[166] Thus, there is a "mutual connection of justice and human felicity."[167]

However, Blackstone noted, it is often difficult to apply the moral law to human affairs. Moral weakness clouds our understanding, preventing us from being objective: "If our reason were always . . . clear and perfect, unruffled by passions, unclouded by prejudice, unimpaired by disease or intemperance, the task would be pleasant and easy."[168]

But every man now finds "the contrary in his own experience; that his reason is corrupt, and his understanding full of ignorance and error."[169] Thus, great effort is now required to discover and articulate legal principles that are just and moral.

Smith (1723–1790)

Adam Smith is the founder of modern economics. His book *The Wealth of Nations* (1776) established his reputation with its realistic and systematic analysis of human economic behavior. Smith attacked the medieval mercantilist system of his day, finding it inherently collusive and harmful to the public's interests. People of the same trade seldom meet together, "even for merriment and diversion," but the conversation "ends in a conspiracy against the public, or in some contrivance to raise prices."[170]

Neither did Smith believe the public benefited from government control of economic activity. "It is the highest impertinence and presumption . . . in kings and ministers to pretend to watch over the economy of private people, and to restrain their expense."[171] Government officials are themselves "always, and without any exception, the greatest spendthrifts in the society."[172] Rulers should "look well after their own expense," and they can "safely trust private people with theirs."[173]

Smith had a realistic view of human motives, which did not expect individuals to behave altruistically—whether in government, guilds, or private business. Instead, people have a strong emotional need for the approval of others. Money and power are not ends in themselves, but means to the ends of social approval:

> [T]o what purpose is all the toil and bustle of this world? What is the end of avarice and ambition, of the pursuit of wealth, of power and pre-eminence? . . . To be observed, to be attended to, to be taken notice of with sympathy, complacency and approbation, are all the advantages which we can propose to derive from it.[174]

Therefore, Smith concluded, national wealth depended upon the proper channeling of this emotional interest in success and approval. People should have these emotional needs met through productive business, not through using guilds or government to control others. Freed from centralized controls, the desire of businesspeople to succeed would lead to competition, which would benefit the public through lower prices and higher quality goods and services. As a result, though individuals are pursuing only their own success, they benefit society by increasing its overall wealth. "He intends only his own gain," but is "led by an invisible hand to promote an end which was no part of his intention"—the wealth of the nation.[175]

Smith's realistic analysis of human motives and mercantilist trade barriers had enormous impact. His writings were obviously not the last word on the subject of economics. He did not foresee the dangers of monopolies. He did not anticipate the need for labor unions and a social safety net. However, he did play a leading role in starting the engines of modern economic growth, bringing untold benefits to the world.

Goethe (1749–1823)

Johann Wolfgang von Goethe was a German poet, dramatist and novelist. Many consider him the last true "Renaissance Man." As a privy councilor at the Duke of Weimar's court, he oversaw major mining, road-building, and irrigation projects. He painted, directed plays, and researched anatomy, botany, and optics. He was also a keen observer of human nature.

Goethe recognized the great human capacity for self-delusion. "One is never deceived; one deceives oneself."[176] No person wishes to be fully known. Everyone has some trait which, openly admitted, "might well cause displeasure."[177]

Goethe did not think much of the exhortation of Greek philosophers to "know thyself." Goethe remarked that it is a requirement "with which nobody complies, or ever will comply."[178] "Altogether, man is a darkened being" who "knows little of the world, and least of himself."[179] Goethe had no wish to know his own motives: "I do not know myself, and God forbid I should."[180] He added: "If I knew myself, I'd run away!"[181]

Madison (1751–1836)

James Madison had a sterling political career, from the Virginia legislature to the U.S. House of Representatives to our nation's fourth president. However, by far, his greatest accomplishment was as the principal author of the Constitution.

After the Revolutionary War, our nation was a loose alliance of states under the Articles of Confederation. The Articles had caused great problems during the Revolution, because they gave Congress no power to tax or draft an army. Congress was at the mercy of the states to voluntarily send soldiers and funds for the war. Afterwards, the Articles were completely unworkable, since they gave no power to establish a common currency or regulate trade with other nations.

However, the nation was extremely nervous about creating a strong national government. Having just fought a bloody war to obtain freedom from an oppressive crown, Americans had no interest in creating a similar tyranny on this side of the Atlantic.

Madison shared the nation's concerns about concentration of power. Principled leaders like Washington and Jefferson could be trusted with power. However, that would not always be the case. Enlightened statesmen would not always be at the helm.

Human nature is selfish, and cannot be entrusted with absolute power.

> [W]hat is government itself but the greatest of all reflections on human nature? If men were angels, no government would be necessary. If angels were to govern men, neither external nor internal controls on government would be necessary.[182]

Clearly, then, a national government would need incentives to control itself. Since there would be no higher secular authority, the controls had to come from within. Power had to be divided. Permanent, competing factions would need the means and the interest to check each other's power.

> [T]he great security against a gradual concentration of the several powers in the same department, consists in giving to those who administer each department, the necessary constitutional means, and personal motives, to resist encroachment of the others. . . . Ambition must be made to counteract ambition.[183]

Madison referred to this concept of checks and balances as the "policy of supplying by opposite and rival interests, the defect of better motives."[184]

Madison incorporated these principles into the Virginia Plan, which became adopted with a few modifications as the U.S. Constitution. That document has been remarkably practical and durable. It is the world's oldest constitution, and has successfully avoided the scourge of dictatorship. It is a tribute to the care taken by Madison. He took the time to purposely design a government around a realistic understanding of human nature.

Jung (1875–1961)

Carl Gustav Jung was one of the world's pioneers in psychology and psychiatry. Trained as a physician, he was strongly influenced by the work of Sigmund Freud. Jung provided the first experimental verification of Freud's concept of repression. Using word-association tests, Jung showed that people were influenced by ideas of which they were unaware.

Jung's experience with psychoanalysis confirmed the significance of the subconscious mind. When a conscious experience proved unacceptable and caused conflict, it was repressed and became unconscious. Jung discovered that neurosis was frequently a symptom of imbalance in the conscious mind, which the unconscious mind was attempting to correct.

Jung also found evidence that much of the subconscious mind represented the "dark" side of the person's personality. Often this dark side manifests itself in dreams as an anonymous sinister figure he referred to as the "shadow." The shadow is hard for most people to face. "No one can become conscious of the shadow without considerable moral effort. To become conscious of it involves recognizing the dark aspects of the personality as present and real."[185]

Toward the end of his life, Jung became increasingly convinced that people routinely repressed evil motives, causing great danger to the world. "We need more understanding of human nature," he said in a 1959 BBC interview, "because the only real danger that exists is man himself." The psyche must be studied "because we are the origin of all coming evil."[186]

Alexander (20th–21st century)

Biologist Richard D. Alexander is professor of evolutionary biology at the University of Michigan. He emphasizes that certain ideas and myths increase the chances for human survival.

In particular, "modern society is filled with myths" about our goodness.[187] These include: "that scientists are humble and devoted truth-seekers; that doctors dedicate their lives to alleviation of suffering; that teachers dedicate their lives to their students; that we are all basically law-abiding, kind, altruistic souls who place everyone's interests before our own."[188]

These myths and self-images can become dangerous to society, though, if we do not carefully examine their accuracy. To the extent they are false, they can "lead us in unwanted directions."[189] The reality about human conduct is less pleasant than the myth: "Only in humans is the major hostile force of life composed of other groups in the same species."[190] Recognizing this reality is crucial to humanity's progress.

Wright (20th–21st century)

Scientist Robert Wright is a contributing editor at *The New Republic*. His recent book *The Moral Animal* examines the biological roots of human morality.

Wright observes that human morality is based on self-interest rather than altruism: "[T]he moral sentiments are used with brutal flexibility, switched on and off in keeping with self-interest."[191]

Wright remarks how little people are aware of this moral selectivity. Human beings are a species "splendid in their array of moral equipment, tragic in their propensity to misuse it, and pathetic in their constitutional ignorance of the misuse."[192]

This ignorance of our motives is based on the universal tendency to see ourselves in a good light:

> One might think that, being rational creatures, we would eventually grow suspicious of our uncannily long string

> of rectitude, our unerring knack for being on the right side of any dispute over credit, or money, or manners, or anything else. Nope. Time and again—whether arguing over a place in line, a promotion we never got, or which car hit which—we are shocked at the blindness of people who dare suggest that our outrage isn't warranted.[193]

Pol Pot (1925–1998)

The modern world is filled with examples of evil people deluding themselves about their moral purity. But surely one of the classic examples is the Cambodian tyrant Pol Pot.

Pol Pot was born to a royal family in Cambodia, which was under French control. At the age of twenty he went to Paris to study science. He was a failure as a student. However, while in Paris, he formed a small network of Cambodian communists. Together, they returned to Cambodia and formed the Khmer Rouge, with Pol Pot as their leader.

In 1975, the Khmer Rouge faction came to power in Cambodia. They began a reign of terror, seeking to "purify" Cambodia from all foreign influences, to depopulate the cities, and to return the country to an agrarian lifestyle. As many as 2 million people died over the next four years from starvation, overwork, and execution.

In 1979, in retaliation for Khmer Rouge attacks, Vietnam overthrew the Cambodian government, forcing Pol Pot into exile. He made many attempts to regain power, but never succeeded.

Pol Pot gave an interview to the Wall Street Journal in 1997. Did he express remorse over the killings, or a feeling of guilt? Not surprisingly, he did not.

Asked whether he wanted to apologize for the suffering he caused, he looked "genuinely confused," stated the reporter. He had the interpreter repeat the question, then answered "No."[194]

"I came to carry out the struggle, not to kill people," Pol Pot said. "Even now . . . you can look at me, am I a savage person? My conscience is clear."[195]

Scriptures

The Hebrew and Christian Scriptures are noteworthy for their realistic view of human nature. The heroes of the Bible are all flawed heroes—people with serious moral failings.[196] Abraham was a liar,[197] and Moses was a murderer;[198] King Solomon was an idolater,[199] and the prophet Isaiah was profane;[200] the apostle Peter was a coward,[201] and the apostle Paul was cruel.[202] They are all examples, though, because they acknowledged their need for forgiveness.

Perhaps the best example is King David, one of the noblest people in Scripture. He earnestly sought after God, examined his own motives, and sought to live a good life. As a youth he experienced privation—first as a humble shepherd, then as a soldier. Under these harsh circumstances, we are not surprised when people take moral shortcuts.

David was eventually crowned king of Israel. He enjoyed success, peace, and prosperity. Yet he did not experience moral perfection. Instead, David committed adultery and murder. As a result of this great moral failure, David saw that his problem was more radical than occasional bad acts; it was inherent in his very nature. "Surely I was sinful at birth, sinful from the time my mother conceived me."[203] Due to his honesty, David sought and received forgiveness for all his sins.[204]

Acknowledging our selfish motives is the first step to forgiveness. Jesus frequently dealt with the Pharisees—a group of religious teachers who believed their moral conduct made them right with God. Jesus told the Pharisees that they were hypocrites—play actors—people pretending to be good.[205] They may have fooled themselves and others, but they had not fooled God, who sees the heart.

Jesus warned people to avoid the hypocrisy of the Pharisees. He told of two people who went to the Temple to pray. One, a Pharisee, thanked God that he was a good man. The other, a reprobate tax collector, simply prayed, "God, have mercy on me, a sinner." The tax collector went home forgiven, not the Pharisee.[206]

Naturally, this kind of teaching offended the Pharisees. However, Jesus did not back down. Instead, he told the Pharisees that they were "blind"—not seeing their own immorality. When the Pharisees objected to this term, Jesus responded that they had made their own choice. "If you were blind, you would not be guilty of sin; but now that you claim you can see, your guilt remains."[207]

Summary

People have an almost infinite capacity to rationalize. We constantly tell ourselves that our motives are pure, when in fact they are selfish. Even our best conduct is, upon close inspection, simply wise or enlightened self-interest.

In chapter 2 we concluded that the moral law punishes all selfish conduct. This creates a mind-boggling problem: if all our conduct is selfish, then every moment we build up new judgment for ourselves. The longer we live, the worse it gets. There appears to be no way to escape. This is a serious, universal dilemma.

Clearly we all need protection from the moral law—we all need forgiveness. We assume this is a simple matter for God. He is good and merciful. Can't he just forgive our sins as a lender can choose to forgive a debt?

However, our problem is more difficult than it first appears. How can God forgive us without ignoring the moral law? If all immoral conduct must be punished, then forgiveness appears to be impossible.

Since the beginning of time, morally serious world religions have attempted to resolve this dilemma. The remaining chapters will examine whether any religions have succeeded. Have any identified a mechanism for God to forgive people while still fully enforcing the moral law?

For Further Reading on Human Nature:

Dawkins, Richard. *The Selfish Gene*. Oxford University Press, 1976.

Degler, Carl. *In Search of Human Nature*. Oxford University Press, 1991.

Hobbes, Thomas. *Human Nature*. Oxford University Press, 1994 reprint.

Hume, David. *A Treatise of Human Nature*. Penguin, 1969 reprint.

Lovejoy, Arthur. *Reflections on Human Nature*. Johns Hopkins Press, 1961.

Myers, David. *The Inflated Self*. Seabury, 1980.

Plantinga, Cornelius. *Not the Way It's Supposed To Be*. Eerdmans, 1995.

Voltaire, François. *Philosophical Dictionary*. Penguin, 1972 reprint.

Watson, Lyall. *Dark Nature*. Harper-Collins, 1995.

4

Good Works Religion?

As you explore the world's religions, you find that most contain strong elements of good works. In many religions, moral conduct is the only specific remedy to the universal dilemma. By living a good life, your good deeds will outweigh your bad deeds.

Does this approach make sense? Does it resolve the universal dilemma? Does it provide a mechanism for forgiveness? Does it allow God to punish all immoral acts?

In this chapter, we will examine three well-established good works religions—Islam, Buddhism, and Sikhism. We will also examine a new variation on good works religion—

the New Age movement. We will see the prominent place they give to morality. We will also see whether they provide a mechanism for transforming moral acts into forgiveness.

Islam

Islam truly deserves its place as one of the world's great religions. Founded by Muhammad in the seventh century C.E., it now is embraced by almost one billion people. Beyond sheer numbers, there is an admirable purity to its teaching—combining a strict monotheism with an equally strict moral code. Finally, at many points in history, Islam has been a great sponsor of art, learning, and culture.

From current events, we are all familiar with the teaching that Muslim martyrs can go straight to heaven. However, that is not the norm. For the average Muslim, heaven is achieved through a moral life. Let us examine what this means.

As we begin to examine Islam, we first notice the religion's name. In Arabic, "Islam" means both "peace" and "submission."[208] Thus, Islam can be defined as "peace . . . by surrendering to God's law."[209] Likewise, the word "Muslim" means a person who surrenders to God's law.[210] Thus, conformity to God's law is the heart of Islam.

The Qur'an (Koran) is the Muslim Bible. It supplements and modifies much of the Hebrew Scriptures (the Old

Testament) and the Christian Scriptures (the New Testament). The Qur'an maintains most of the moral principles of the Hebrew and Christian Scriptures, including the Ten Commandments.

To the Jewish and Christian moral teachings, the Qur'an adds a special focus on economic issues. For example, a tax is levied on the wealthy, to be spent on the poor and needy.[211] Also, detailed inheritance laws require shares for daughters as well as sons.[212] This was a significant reform in Arab society, where women were often disinherited.

The Qur'an emphasizes God's moral justice. All our decisions in this life, whether good or bad, are rewarded in the next life. "Your Lord will surely reward all men according to their deeds. He has knowledge of all their actions."[213]

God's scrutiny extends beyond our outward actions to our inward motives. He knows our "innermost thoughts."[214] He knows what is in our "hearts."[215] He rejects outwardly good works done with bad motives, such as giving charity to people we despise.[216]

Throughout your life, an angel stands by your side. Your moral choices are written in a personal "book." Whether good or bad, the angels "record it all."[217]

On the Day of Judgment, each person is told, "Read your book; your own soul is sufficient as a reckoner against you this day."[218] Those who have done wrong will be dismayed at the contents of their book. "Woe to us! What can this book mean? It omits nothing small or great: all is noted down!"[219]

We will then be judged, based upon this detailed record of good and bad conduct. There will be a "weighing the deeds."[220] Those whose good deeds are "heavy" will be rewarded.[221] Those whose good deeds are "light" will be punished—they have "ruined their souls."[222]

Deeds done for short-term, earthly benefit are judged severely. "Shall we tell you of those who are the greatest losers in terms of their deeds? Those whose whole effort has been lost [in pursuit of] this life, but they think they have performed prodigies."[223]

Thus, the Qur'an sets forth a rigorous system of moral justice. All of our bad deeds will be punished, including outwardly good deeds done for bad motives. All of our good deeds will be rewarded, if they outweigh the bad.

How does Islam handle the problem of human motivation? If all of our deeds are selfish, won't we all suffer punishment? Islam provides no clear answer to this problem. The Qur'an suggests that, due to God's mercy, believers will not be fully punished. (This approach is analyzed in the next chapter, on the "religious exception.")

Therefore, Islam's rigorous teachings on morality and judgment highlight, but do not resolve, the universal dilemma. If every selfish deed is recorded and judged, then the human race is truly in trouble.

Buddhism

In recent years, Buddhism has experienced explosive growth in the United States. The reasons given for its popularity are many. But clearly one reason is its plain, practical statements of moral principles.

The teachings of the Buddha (Siddhartha Gautama) and his disciples are contained in the Tripitaka ("Three Baskets"). These are three book or collections—the Discourses, the Disciplines, and the Higher Teachings.

Buddhism has a strong doctrine of moral cause and effect. Our thoughts, words, and deeds have consequences ("karma") either for happiness or for suffering. Good or "meritorious" karma leads to good health, long life, wealth, power, and pleasure. It ultimately leads to rebirth as a higher being or, perhaps, to the heaven of Nirvana.

Bad or "demeritorious" karma has the opposite effect. It leads to poor health, short life, poverty, weakness, and suffering. It ultimately leads to rebirth as a subhuman being.

Buddhism has a heaven—Nirvana. There, desire and suffering end, and the soul experiences freedom from future rebirth, old age, and death.

Nirvana is achieved by following the Eightfold Path: (1) right views, (2) right intent, (3) right speech, (4) right conduct, (5) right livelihood, (6) right effort, (7) right attentiveness, and (8) right concentration.[224] These eight virtues can be summarized as follows:

1. "Right views" or "right understanding" is seeing the Eightfold Path as the way to end desire and suffering.[225]

2. "Right intent" or "right mindedness" is thought free from lust, ill will, and cruelty.[226]

3. "Right speech" avoids lying, gossiping, harsh language, and idle talk.[227]

4. "Right conduct" or "right action" avoids murder, stealing, and adultery.[228]

5. "Right livelihood" or "right living" is work or employment that does not require wrong conduct.[229]

6. "Right effort" is the effort to avoid and overcome evil desires, and to develop and maintain an enlightened mindset.[230]

7. "Right attentiveness" is contemplating the body, feeling, the mind, and phenomena.[231]

8. "Right concentration" is fixing the mind on a single object—one of the four objects of right attentiveness.[232]

By following these eight moral disciplines, then, suffering and desire are extinguished and Nirvana achieved. It is a straightforward program for achieving heaven through moral effort. In that sense, it is much like Islam. However, unlike Islam, the Buddhist heaven is not a reward by God for good works—it is the natural consequence of good works, with no divine intervention required.

The Buddhist remedy of good works falls short, however, if human nature is fundamentally flawed. If selfishness is inherent in human nature, then we will never be free from desire. By living a wise life, our suffering will be diminished. However, at the root, we will still be the same selfish people. We will still desire to please ourselves. This will continue to produce bad karma. We will continue to fall further into debt.

Sikhism

Most of us have heard of the Sikh religion in only one context—media accounts of terrorist acts by "Sikh extremists." However, like most religious terrorists, the Sikh militants are a small minority of their religion. It is intellectually dishonest to paint the entire religion with the same broad brush. Let us take a closer look.

The Sikh religion originated in the Punjab, a region currently divided between Pakistan and India. It began around 1500 C.E. with a small group of disciples of the Guru Nanak dedicated to seeking the presence of God. Over the years they grew in numbers and became a distinct community.

Initially, the Sikhs were lead by a series of ten Gurus or teachers. In 1708, following the death of the final Guru, Gobind

Singh, the writings of the Gurus were collected into the Sikh Scriptures, the Guru Granth.

The Sikhs teach that people are by nature proud and selfish, with a corrupting passion for the world and its pleasures. This corruption is known as *haumai*.[233] It blinds us to the true nature of life. Even religious rituals and creeds can be expressions of this pride and selfishness. The person who is lost in this proud selfishness is "drowned without water."[234]

For the Sikhs, liberation from this selfishness and pride comes gradually, from a prolonged focus on God. The heart and the will must focus on God, not on self. By placing God in the center of life, the individual is gradually freed from selfishness and pride. It is a five-stage process. Ultimate deliverance is found in the fifth stage—*sach khand* or the "realm of truth."[235]

The Sikh system of salvation certainly has much to make it attractive. It combines belief in God with an accurate assessment of human nature. The focus on God rather than self, no doubt, produces substantial moral improvement.

However, the Sikh program requires many years to produce an unselfish soul. What happens to all of the selfish and immoral acts committed during that process? Alas, like Islam and Buddhism, the Sikhs have no mechanism to allow these acts to be punished. God is required to ignore all the prior moral law violations.

New Age

Compared to the other religions in this chapter, the New Age movement is a newcomer, originating during the 1960s American counterculture. Although it draws strains of thought from many religions, it represents a modern synthesis that appeals to the modern western mind. It represents a "new age" of people who take the best from all world religions.

The New Age movement is not a formal religion. It has no sacred writings or traditions. It has no formal institutions. It is, rather, a loose collection of autonomous groups and philosophies. Thus it is in some ways impervious to rigorous analysis. However, there are two general characteristics we can identify and critique.

First, the New Age movement has enthusiastically adopted the Hindu and Buddhist concept of *karma*.[236] As noted in chapter 2, karma is a strict moral law, visiting on people the consequences of their conduct, whether good or bad. In this area, then, the New Age movement is similar to most other world religions.

Second, the movement does not like the concept of judgment following death. It sounds too harsh to modern ears—eternal reward of punishment based on only a few decades of actions and decisions. Thus, New Age adherents have also adopted the eastern concept of reincarnation.[237] Reincarnation gives people many lifetimes to "get it right." If we make some bad choices in this lifetime, we can make up for it in future lives.

In fact, though, reincarnation simply multiplies the problems inherent in good works religions. If all of our actions are selfish and violate the moral law, then the last thing we want is multiple lives. If we live for hundreds of years, we will simply acquire an immense debt of bad karma. Therefore, if we start with a realistic view of human nature, reincarnation is bad news, not good news. It worsens, rather than relieves, the universal dilemma of judgment.

Summary

Good works religions have much to commend them. They encourage moral seriousness and moral purity. They take the human heart away from short-term, selfish concerns. They encourage a long-term view, where people consider the consequences of evil actions. In short, they lead to a more enlightened and less damaging form of self-interest.

However, a system of good works does not resolve the universal dilemma. It may reduce the seriousness of our moral law violations. But it does not eliminate the selfish motives underlying even our best deeds. Thus, every day we live we produce further moral law violations. Our "good works" pile up the unpaid debt of punishment. The pile keeps getting larger; the debt keeps getting greater.

Therefore, a different approach is required—one that gets us beyond the judgment of the moral law. In the next chapter, we will examine religious practices designed to sever the connection between immoral acts and personal judgment.

For Further Reading on Good Works Religions:

Ali, Maulana Muhammad. *The Religion of Islam*. Ahmadiyya Anjuman Isha'at Islam, 1990.

Eerdman's Handbook to the World's Religions. 1994.

Goddard, Dwight, ed. *A Buddhist Bible*. Beacon, 1994.

Halverson, Dean, ed. *The Compact Guide to World Religions*. Bethany House Publishers, 1996.

Harper-Collins Dictionary of Religions. 1995.

Occhiogrosso, Peter. *The Joy of Sects*. Doubleday, 1996.

Bowker, John, ed. *Oxford Dictionary of World Religions*. 1997.

World Religions. Macmillan, 1987.

5

Religious Ritual: A Religious Exception to Judgment?

IF GOOD WORKS cannot overcome our moral deficit with God, is there another way? Is there a "religious exception" to the moral law? Is there a religious method or ritual by which we can escape the stern grip of moral cause and effect?

This chapter will analyze the efficacy of four common religious rituals: cleansing, enlightenment, sacrificial gifts, and animal sacrifice.

Cleansing (Shinto)

Shinto is the indigenous Japanese religious tradition. It is, to this day, the dominant religion in Japan. It has no known founder, and its precise origins remain somewhat of a mystery.

The term *shinto* is based upon the Chinese words *shen* ("divine being") and *tao* ("way").[238] The Chinese coined the term in the sixth century C.E. to distinguish the traditional Japanese religion from Buddhism, the more secular religion that came to Japan from China.

Shinto has no sacred scriptures and no fixed system of doctrine. It has, instead, well-established traditions embedded in Japanese culture. These traditions include the belief in *musubi*, the harmony of nature, and *makoto*, truthfulness.

Shinto stresses gratefulness for the blessings of heaven. Humans receive life from ancestors and the gods. People are born essentially good, but can be defiled by immoral choices. Once our defilement is removed, our original purity can be restored.

Thus, a central component of the Shinto religion is the removal of defilement. This involves different levels of ritual. For example, the biannual Shinto ceremony of Oho-harahi is similar to a rite of confession; it centers on a priest's recitation of a complete list of possible sins or impurities.[239]

Misogi is an act of ritual purification. Water is poured over the body, usually at a river or seashore. The ritual symbolizes the cleansing of pollution from the body.[240]

Purification is also required as the worshipper approaches a Shinto shrine. At the shrine's entrance stands the *torii*, or gateway, marking the boundary between the sacred and the secular. As people enter, they must wash their hands and rinse their mouths in the absolution basin.

A person with a guilty conscience may go to a shrine to recite a prayer of repentance. For great guilt, a person may perform a "hundredfold" repentance, or *ohyakudo*. Some shrines have two stone markers for this purpose; the guilty person walks back and forth a hundred times between the two stones, repeating a phrase of repentance.[241]

The Shinto religion's emphasis upon the need for confession and cleansing is commendable. It shows an awareness of moral guilt before the divine. It shows the need for forgiveness.

However, we must ask about the effectiveness of the Shinto purification method. Does rinsing with water actually rinse away immorality? Does the water somehow absorb God's judgment?

Unfortunately, outward cleansing does not resolve the universal dilemma. It does not provide a mechanism by which God can punish the immoral conduct. It is, at most, an acknowledgement of need—the universal need for forgiveness.

Enlightenment (Hindu)

The Hindu religion seeks another form of escape from judgment—escape to a mental or spiritual plane apart from the judgment of karma.

The Hindus have a strong doctrine of karma. A person's actions in this life, whether good or bad, have consequences in the next life. Through reincarnation, a person moves "up" or "down" in a new life, depending upon the person's moral conduct in the last life. If the last life was predominantly good, then he or she is reincarnated in a higher caste. If the last life was predominantly bad, then reincarnation will be a lower caste of human or even as an animal.

Even if this were true, it would not solve the universal dilemma. Since all of our conduct is selfish, none of it is good. Each time we were reincarnated we would live at a lower level. There would be no upward mobility.

The Hindu religion implicitly acknowledges this problem. The Hindu Scriptures provide for *moksa*—a release or escape from the endless cycle of reincarnation. Moksa is achieved principally through enlightenment about the true nature of reality.[242]

The individual self is, ultimately, an illusion. In reality, we are all extensions of Brahman, an impersonal oneness that is beyond distinctions. Through prolonged self-denial and meditation, a person can be freed from the illusion of individuality. The person enters the state of enlightenment, where karma cannot reach. This enlightenment takes even the "foulest of sinners" and carries them, like a raft, over all their sins.[243]

The Hindus are to be commended for seeing the need to be freed from moral judgment—from karma. Like the ritual Shinto washings, the doctrine of moksa represents an acknowledgement of the need for forgiveness. However, does moksa provide a true mechanism for judgment and forgiveness?

Moksa detaches the person from moral consequences. It leaves those consequences essentially "free floating" in this world, never to be judged. It thus fails the "full judgment" test.

To use an everyday analogy, moksa is like declaring bankruptcy. In bankruptcy, the court declares a person's financial debts forgiven and gives the person a fresh start. Thus, bankruptcy is good news for the debtor. However, it is bad news for the creditors—the people who lent the money—because the debts are not actually repaid.

Bankruptcy is a necessary evil in today's economy. A person who declares bankruptcy has a chance to become a productive citizen—a positive impact on the economy. This social good outweighs the harm caused to individual creditors.

However, we expect more from heaven. We want moral perfection, not moral compromise. We want and need perfect justice—the full judgment of evil. Moral bankruptcy is unacceptable.

Sacrificial Gifts (Taoism)

In many traditional religions, a person will relinquish an item of value to resolve moral guilt. Such a sacrificial gift, the person hopes, will compensate for the offense and avert moral judgment.

Sacrificial giving is a component of Taoism, the traditional religion of China. The Tao religion has a strong moral focus, seeking to liberate people from mundane activities, to focus on permanent truths and values.

When the people fall short of this goal, or the community is facing some type of natural disaster, the local priest seeks to renew their relationship with heaven. The method for reconciliation is the ritual of *chiao.*[244] The priest makes offerings of pure food—wine, cakes, fruit, or tea. The priest then prays for forgiveness, and for renewal of heaven's protections.

Such an offering is a good first step, if it represents an acknowledgment of guilt. However, beyond that, it provides no means for God to punish the immoral act. Moreover, as with other "good works," the sacrifice is itself motivated by self-interest. Thus, the act of making a sacrificial gift, in and of itself, violates the moral law. Clearly, something further is required.

Animal Sacrifice

Reviewing the above religious rituals, we could lose heart. The picture is bleak. It appears nothing we can do will neutralize moral judgment. However, through the gloom, we see rays of hope from an unlikely source—animal sacrifice.

To the modern mind, animal sacrifices seem somewhat barbaric. However, prior to Christianity, animal sacrifices were an almost universal religious practice. Biologist and naturalist

Lyall Watson observes that animal sacrifice is "one of the cornerstones of human history."[245] He connects the practice to the universal sense of moral guilt, and the universal desire for moral justice. "We feel that those who do good, deserve reward; and those who do bad, deserve punishment."[246] We overcome the fear of punishment "by seeking a scapegoat and offering this up in our place."[247]

A long-standing tradition of animal sacrifice is found in the Nuer tribe in Africa. The Nuer are a cattle herding people in the Sudan. They believe that God, the creator of the universe, is morally perfect.[248] God rewards good acts and punishes bad acts.[249] To avert God's punishment, the Nuer will sacrifice an ox as a substitute. The guilty person consecrates the ox by rubbing ashes from the family byre onto the animal's back. The Nuer explain that this rite places all the evil in the person's heart onto the beast. When the ox is killed, the evil flows into the earth with the blood.[250]

Thus, animal sacrifice introduces a concept commonly known as "atonement"—the punishment of a substitute. This is clearly a step forward, beyond other religious rituals. It suggests that God can separate the evil from the person. The immoral person can be forgiven, while the immorality is separately punished.

However, upon closer inspection, animal sacrifice does not satisfy the requirement of full moral judgment. There are at least three defects: (1) animals are not morally equivalent to humans, (2) animals are not volunteers and thus cannot accept punishment for another, and (3) animals are not immortal and thus cannot be a perpetual substitute.

Summary

Religious ritual is a step beyond good works religion. There is an acknowledgment of the inadequacy of good works, and the need for mercy. Animal sacrifice is arguably two steps beyond good works religion, suggesting a substitute punishment of immorality.

Thus, religious rituals seem to point the way to a solution. However, they do not actually provide the solution. Apparently, something more radical is required.

The human race has a very practical need—the need for forgiveness. Yet we have found no mechanism to provide forgiveness.

The need for forgiveness is like a great thirst, a thirst that must be quenched. Yet it appears this thirst is unquenchable.

In our hearts we know this cannot be. We admit our need. God would not abandon us. God *must* have a solution.

In the next chapter, we will see if Christianity succeeds where other religions have failed. Does it describe a real mechanism for forgiveness? Can it quench the unquenchable thirst?

For Further Reading on Religious Ritual:

Bhagavad Gita.

Halverson, Dean C., ed. *The Compact Guide to World Religions.* Bethany, 1996.

Eerdmans' Handbook to the World's Religions. 1994.

Eliade, Mircea. *Patterns in Comparative Religion.* Sheed and Ward, 1958.

Evans-Pritchard, Edward. *Nuer Religion.* Clarendon, 1956.

Kulandran, Sabapathy. *Grace in Christianity and Hinduism.* Lutterworth, 1964.

Earhart, H. Byron, ed. *Religious Traditions of the World.* Harper-Collins, 1993.

Parrinder, Geoffrey, ed. *World Religions from Ancient History to the Present.* Hamlyn, 1983.

6

Christianity: The Radical Solution?

SERIOUS PROBLEMS may require radical solutions. That appears to be the case with the universal dilemma.

The human race needs forgiveness. Yet, to be blunt, traditional religious solutions are failures. Good works and religious rituals are totally inadequate for the task. Something more radical is required. Otherwise, realistically, our prospects for the next life are quite bleak.

Does Christianity have the answer? Is it like other religions, offering some mixture of good works and religious ritual? Or does it describe a true, logical solution to the universal dilemma? In this chapter we will examine this last hope for the human race.

We start with the Hebrew Scriptures (Old Testament), which clarify the need for a perfect substitute sacrifice. We finish with the Christian Scriptures (New Testament), which claim that God himself provided the sacrifice.

Cain and Abel

Not surprisingly, the Scriptures begin by affirming the practice of animal sacrifice. From the earliest human generations, we see God encouraging the mindset of substitute punishment.

The story of Cain and Abel is fairly well known. Cain and Abel were brothers. In fact they were the "founding brothers," the first sons of Adam and Eve, the parents of the human race. Thus, they should have felt a deep kinship and friendship. In fact, Cain became so jealous of Abel that he murdered him.

What was the source of their conflict? What sparked Cain's intense jealousy of Abel? (This is the part of the story we often brush over.) It all started with two different approaches to religious ritual.

Cain and Abel knew they were not right with God, and they prepared two different sacrifices. Cain offered a sacrificial gift—part of the harvest he had produced as a farmer. Abel offered an animal sacrifice. God accepted Abel's animal sacrifice, but not Cain's sacrificial gift. This is what so enraged Cain—the rejection of his "good works" approach to God.[251]

God's design here was clearly benevolent. He wanted to provide early guidance to the human race about the need for a substitute sacrifice. He wanted to discourage a shallow approach to religion, where an occasional payment to God was thought to balance the books.

But Cain closed his heart—to God, to his brother Abel, and to his own need for forgiveness. Cain could have analyzed God's response, seen his need for a substitute sacrifice, and followed Abel's lead.

Instead of acknowledging his need, though, Cain killed his brother. Rather than addressing his own faults, Cain blamed another.[252] As a result, Cain's name lives to this day as a symbol of infamy and treachery.

So the story of Cain and Abel teaches us two related lessons. First, substitute sacrifice is the correct approach to God. Second, we should be quick to admit our faults, rather than projecting blame onto others.

Passover

Israel's exodus from Egypt is one of the most important events in the Hebrew Scriptures, and in world history. The Jewish people simultaneously received their independence from Egypt and their liberation from slavery. It was like combining the United States' Declaration of Independence (independence from Britain) with our Emancipation Proclamation (liberty for slaves).

However, we should not forget the sequence of events. Before the exodus came a sacrifice, the Passover.

According to the Scriptures, Pharaoh had stubbornly refused to grant freedom to the Hebrews. Moses had made many demands of Pharaoh, and God had sent many natural disasters to Egypt, but Pharaoh was determined to maintain their slavery.[253]

Finally, God sent the angel of death, who killed all the firstborn children in Egypt. Following this great calamity, Pharaoh relented, and Israel was freed.[254]

Was God unjust in causing these deaths? Not at all! First, all people must die; God has the right, as our Creator, to choose the timing. Second, the cruelty of slavery is a serious breach of the moral law; God has the right, as our Judge, to punish nations for their sins. Third, all people are immoral and subject to full punishment in the next life; an early death in this life is less severe than the judgment coming in the next.

If the Egyptian deaths were just, then why were the Jewish firstborn spared? The Jews were living in Egypt. Doesn't justice require impartial judgment? This is why the Passover sacrifice was so important. God had provided the Hebrews with a way to escape the judgment of death.

Each Hebrew household had to kill, cook, and eat a lamb. The lamb's blood was painted over the door of the house. When the Angel of Death saw this blood, it would pass over the house, and spare its inhabitants.[255] (Thus, the lamb sacrificed was known as the "Passover" lamb.)

Through the Passover sacrifice, the Jewish people were spared the judgment of death. The next morning, Pharaoh freed them from bondage.[256]

To this day, every year, observant Jews celebrate the Passover. The center of this holy day is a meal of lamb. The story of the exodus is retold during that meal.

Which was more significant for the Jewish people—the deliverance from slavery or the deliverance from death? The name of the holy day suggests the answer. The name is "Passover," not "Exodus." The focus is on the sacrificial lamb.

Thus, political freedom is important, but freedom from God's judgment is essential. And judgment is avoided by atonement—by a substitute sacrifice.

Day of Atonement

The annual sacrifice of a Passover lamb was insufficient to secure forgiveness. Israel's worship of God required constant animal sacrifices. Daily sacrifices of sheep and other animals were required to purify the Temple in Jerusalem, and those who worshipped therein.

However, even these daily sacrifices were insufficient to purify the nation. According to the Scriptures, an annual Day of Atonement ("Yom Kippur") was also required.

On the Day of Atonement, the nation rested from work and fasted. The focus was on the High Priest, who acted on behalf of the people. He first sacrificed a bull to make atonement for his own sins.[257] He then approached the Most Holy Place in the Temple—the chamber with the Ark of the Covenant, containing the Ten Commandments.

Standing before the Most Holy Place, the High Priest offered two goats to atone for the nation's sins. The first goat was killed as a traditional offering, and its blood spilled on top of the Ark of the Covenant.[258] (This top was called the Mercy Seat, because God's presence rested there to provide mercy to the people.)[259]

The second goat is the most interesting. Its name is known to this day—the "scape goat." The High Priest laid his hands on the goat's head and confessed all of the nation's immorality. He then sent the goat into the desert, carrying all of the nation's sins away from the Temple.[260]

The use of two goats reinforces the impression that animal sacrifices are inadequate. If the first goat's death secured forgiveness for the nation, then why was a scapegoat required? Why was either goat required, when the people already had the daily sacrifices and the annual Passover sacrifice?

As noted in the last chapter, animal sacrifices do not seem adequate to atone for human sins. Animals are not morally equivalent to humans, and they are not volunteers. Moreover, given the human race's endless supply of selfish acts, an endless number of animal sacrifices would be required.

What we need, it seems, is a substitute that (1) is morally equivalent to humans, and (2) has an infinite capacity to absorb our punishment. To these we should probably add a third requirement: (3) this substitute should be free from personal immorality, so as not to require personal punishment.

Isaiah

Isaiah was one of Israel's greatest prophets. He lived from approximately 740 – 681 B.C.E. During a long public career, he proclaimed both judgment and forgiveness to the Jewish people, and to the world.

Israel was the greatest, most moral nation in the world. Yet, according to Isaiah, the people fell far short of God's standards. The nation was "loaded with guilt" and subject to God's judgment.[261] Animal sacrifices would not save them.[262]

There was hope for Israel and the world. But it would not be through human moral perfection, or through animal sacrifices. The hope was that God would provide another way.

Isaiah predicted the coming of two mysterious people. The first person was fully God and fully human. He would be born as a "child," yet he would be called "Mighty God." He would be a Jewish king, yet be a light to the whole world. His reign would be peaceful and eternal.[263]

At first glance, this God-man would seem to answer all of humanity's problems. He would bring world peace. Yet Isaiah predicted the coming of another person—a suffering servant.

This second person would have a hard life. He would be rejected by the people, and would be put to death. Yet somehow his suffering and death would act as a substitute for us. He would be pierced for our transgressions, not his own. He would be crushed for our iniquities. Our punishment would be upon him. We have all gone astray, yet God would lay our immorality upon him. He would be like a sacrificial lamb. His death would atone for our guilt.[264]

This second person has most of the qualities we need. As a man, he would be morally equivalent to us. He would apparently be morally innocent, and so could receive judgment on our behalf. Yet could one man be a substitute for all people? Wouldn't he need to be infinite and eternal? Wouldn't he need to have the qualities of the first person—the God-man? Don't these two people have to, in fact, be the same person? Isaiah does not answer this question.

John the Baptist

Around 25 C.E., a new Hebrew prophet emerged. John came seven centuries after Isaiah, yet had a similar message. The nation of Israel was guilty, and needed forgiveness.

John called all people to be baptized in water, as a sign of the need for moral cleansing. This cleansing ritual disturbed the religious leaders of his day. It implied that the traditional animal sacrifices were insufficient. It insinuated that people were still morally unclean.[265]

John did not claim that water baptism was the solution. He was preparing the way for another person. This other person would be superior to John, and would bring about real moral cleansing. He would provide the reality that John's baptism merely symbolized.[266]

When John disclosed this other person's identity, he further annoyed the religious leaders. This other person was Jesus, the humble carpenter-teacher from the small town of Nazareth. Jesus had no special credentials or training; he had no wealth or position. How could he provide moral cleansing superior to water baptism and animal sacrifices?

John did not have the full answer to this challenge. However, John had a partial answer. Jesus was somehow the "Lamb of God, who takes away the sin of the world."[267]

Jesus

Most of us are somewhat familiar with the life of Jesus, as presented in the Christian Scriptures. He was fully God and fully human.[268] He lived a humble and sinless life. He worked as a carpenter until about age thirty, when he began to teach and to challenge the religious establishment.[269]

After nearly three years of teaching, Jesus had thousands of followers. Threatened by his success, the religious and political leaders had him executed through crucifixion.[270] Three days later, to the surprise of his followers, he was no longer dead. He appeared to them fully alive.[271]

Jesus then explained what had happened. His death was for others—not himself. He had conquered death on our behalf. He had taken the full blunt of God's judgment upon himself. Forgiveness was now possible, in reality, for all people.[272]

This, in a nutshell, is what the Christian Scriptures say about Jesus. The claims are startling. Sincere people have struggled over the implications. Could God really become a man? If he did, would he have only come to teach and to die? Could he not have brought peace to the world?

These important questions cannot be fully addressed here. For the inquiring reader, the suggested books at the end of this chapter discuss many such interesting issues.

The question here is a simpler one: **would it work?** If the Christian Scriptures are accurate, would the universal dilemma be solved? If God became a man, could he be judged in our place? Would he be the perfect sacrifice?

As previously noted, the ideal sacrifice would be (1) fully human and thus, morally equivalent to us; (2) personally without fault; and (3) eternal and infinite, to be able to take all human punishment.

If the Christian Scriptures are correct, then Jesus fulfills all three requirements. He was fully human, sharing in our weakness and our sufferings. He was morally and personally without fault—perfect. He was fully God, as confirmed by his overcoming of death.

Thus, at last, a religion has been found that gives full weight to the moral law. Christianity agrees that all immoral acts must be punished. However, it also describes a full solution to the need for forgiveness.

Are the Christian Scriptures historically accurate? That again is beyond the scope of this book. It is a legitimate topic for inquiry, and there are many excellent books on the subject.

Skeptical scholars generally put the burden of proof on the Christian. They argue that the Christian Scriptures should be assumed false—unless there is independent evidence that shows them to be true.

We take the opposite approach—the Christian Bible should be presumed accurate, unless it can be proven false. It alone describes a solution to the universal dilemma. Thus, the burden of proof rests on the skeptics.

Personal Choice

If Christianity is true, then it's incredibly good news. God has resolved the universal dilemma. He has provided a legitimate way of escape from moral judgment. He took upon himself the judgment for each immoral act and every wrongdoing, including yours and mine. Thus, God can forgive us without compromising the moral law.

Is this forgiveness automatic? Will all people be forgiven, or only those who want forgiveness?

According to the Christian Scriptures, forgiveness is readily available—but the decision rests upon each individual. We can admit our need for mercy and receive forgiveness. Or, we can decline our need for mercy and receive justice. The choice is between mercy and justice.[273]

Justice sounds appealing at first. Who could oppose justice? If we go to court, we want the judge to decide our case on the merits. When this life is over—don't we want *the* Judge to evaluate our life on the merits?

For all the reasons presented in this book, the answer is a resounding "No!" We don't want justice. For sinful, immoral people like us, justice means judgment. That is not a rational choice.

Thus, while justice may appeal to our egos, we must resist. We need mercy, not justice. This means admitting our need for forgiveness.

Jesus told a story that illustrates this choice. Two men went to the temple to pray. The first was a religious leader, and the second was a tax collector. The religious leader thanked God that he was not sinful like other people—robbers, evildoers, and adulterers. The tax collector would not even look up to heaven, but could only pray, "God, have mercy on me, a sinner." The tax collector went home forgiven, Jesus taught, but the religious leader did not.[274]

Thus, according to the Scriptures, God will answer a sincere prayer and plea for mercy. But . . . He will also judge us on our merits (based on our *moral goodness*) if we insist. The choice is ours—yours and mine.

Next Step

Many people, theoretically, accept the need for God's mercy and forgiveness, but go no further. Christianity is viewed simply as a heavenly "fire insurance policy," keeping one from judgment. They see it as a way to escape judgment from God, but they show no gratitude to Him, nor do they show any moral improvement.

If you, the reader, are considering this "fire insurance" approach, please reconsider. We believe that is a dangerous and harmful path for at least four reasons.

First, we submit that such an approach is inherently insincere. To be forgiven you must honestly admit your guilt.

A truthful person cannot admit guilt and at the same time suppress it. To admit guilt awakens your conscience to the wrongs you had previously ignored. An awakened conscience also motivates you to seek moral improvement, to avoid future feelings of guilt. Without such a sincere confession of guilt, you cannot expect a real forgiveness.

Second, moral improvement in your life is beneficial. The moral law punishes bad acts and rewards good acts. Having awakened your conscience to the full scope of the moral law, God will not leave you hanging. He will help you root out selfish motives and make genuine moral progress. The moral law will increasingly become second nature. It will lead you to a happier life, both for you and for those who depend upon you.

Third, simple decency requires gratitude for gifts—especially those that are costly to the giver. Forgiveness and the removal of guilt was a costly gift for God—infinitely costly. Jesus, by his death, paid the eternal debt that we could not pay. He was under no obligation to go to the cross. He took pity on us in our weakness. To turn your back on him now would be indecent.

Fourth, history records many shameful acts by people who claimed to be Christians, but lacked an awakened conscience. The Crusades and slavery are two obvious examples, but there are countless others. We submit that these horrid evils are vastly outweighed by the good done by true Christians who made genuine commitments to God. They founded most of the world's hospitals and universities, fought to abolish slavery, and were leading promoters of human rights. Social improvements, initiated by Christians, are an outward proof of genuine, internal forgiveness and changed hearts.

In short, Christianity is not for hypocrites. It is for morally serious people. An awakened conscience is necessary to receive the gift of forgiveness. That same awakened conscience leads inevitably to moral change. The moral law points the way to forgiveness and to life.

So what are you waiting for?

For Further Reading on Christianity:

Athanasius. *On the Incarnation.* (St. Vladimir's Seminary Press, 1996).

Carroll, Vincent and Shiflett, David. *Christianity on Trial.* (Encounter, 2002).

Chesterton, G. K. *Orthodoxy.* (Image Books, 1990).

Kennedy, D. James. *What If Jesus Had Never Been Born?* (Thomas Nelson, 1994).

Lewis, C.S. *Mere Christianity.* (Macmillan, 1943).

Schaeffer, Edith. *Christianity Is Jewish.* (Tyndale, 1975).

Sproul, R. C. *Reasons to Believe.* (Zondervan, 1978).

Strobel, Lee. *The Case for Christ.* (Zondervan, 1998).

Strobel, Lee. The Case for Faith. (Zondervan, 2000).

Zacharias, Ravi. *Jesus Among Other Gods.* (Word, 2001).

Notes

1. Paul Davies, *God and the New Physics* (New York: Simon & Schuster 1983), pp. 3-42, 142-43.
2. Paul Davies, *The Mind of God* (New York: Simon & Schuster 1992), p. 150.
3. Ibid., p. 199.
4. Mircea Eliade, *Essential Sacred Writings From Around the World* (Harper San Francisco 1967), pp. 12-13.
5. Philip Novak, *The World's Wisdom* (Harper San Francisco 1995), p. 345.
6. Eliade, *Essential Sacred Writings*, pp. 11, 13.
7. Ibid., p. 84.
8. Sir Wallis Budge, *Egyptian Religion* (Barnes & Noble reprint 1994), p. 22. Sir Budge was the Keeper of the Eqyptian antiquities in the British Museum.

9. Ibid.
10. Ibid., p. 25.
11. Ibid., p. 26.
12. Ibid., p. 27.
13. Ibid., at pp. 27-28.
14. Aristotle, The Metaphysics, Hugh Lawson-Tancred, trans. (London: Penguin 1998), p. 380.
15. Ibid., pp. 373-75.
16. Eliade, Essential Sacred Writings, p. 6.
17. Ibid., pp. 6-7.
18. Ibid., pp. 7-11.
19. Ibid., pp. 5-6.
20. Quoted in Morris Kline, *Mathematics: The Loss of Certainty* (Oxford University Press 1980), p. 31.
21. Quoted in Nancy R. Pearcey and Charles B. Thaxton, *The Soul of Science* (Wheaton: Crossway 1994), p. 28.
22. Fred Hereen, *Show Me God* (Wheeling: Searchlight 1995), pp. 268-297.
23. *Voltaire on Religion: Selected Writings*, K.W. Applegate trans. (New York: Ungar 1974), pp. 47-48.
24. Quoted in Arthur C. McGiffert, *Protestant Thought Before Kant* (London: Duckworth: 1919), pp. 244-45.
25. Matthew Josephson, *Edison* (New York: John Wiley 1992), p. 439.
26. Ibid., p. 418.
27. Robert Jastrow, *God and the Astronomers*, 2d ed. (New York: Norton 1992), p. 53.
28. Frederick Hoyle, quoted in *Religion and the Scientists*, Mervyn Stockwood ed. (London: SCM 1959), p. 82.

29. Frederick Hoyle, *The Intelligent Universe* (London: Michael Joseph 1983), p. 218.
30. Frederick Hoyle, quoted in Fred Heeren, *Show Me God* (Wheeling: Searchlight 1995), p. 179.
31. Stephen Hawking, *A Brief History of Time* (New York: Bantam 1988), pp. 122-23.
32. Ibid., p. 125.
33. Ibid.
34. Ibid.
35. Ibid.
36. 1 Corinthians 2:7 (God's purposes "before time began").
37. Genesis 1:1 ("In the beginning God created the heavens and the earth"); Hebrews 11:3 ("the universe was formed at God's command").
38. Genesis 1:31 ("God saw all that he had made, and it was very good"); Isaiah 45:18 (God "fashioned and made the earth" and "formed it to be inhabited").
39. Colossians 1:17 (In Him "all things hold together"); Psalm 36:6 (God "preserves both man and beast").
40. Psalm 9:7 ("The LORD reigns forever"); Psalm 135:6 ("The LORD does whatever pleases him"); Isaiah 40:23 ("He brings princes to naught and reduces the rulers of this world to nothing").
41. Proverbs 15:3 ("The eyes of the LORD are everywhere, keeping watch on the wicked and the good"); Psalm 147:5 (God's understanding "has no limit").
42. Psalm 139:4 ("Before a word is on my tongue you know it completely, O LORD").

43. Matthew 10:30 ("even the very hairs of your head are all numbered").
44. Deuteronomy 5:7 ("You shall have no other gods before me").
45. Romans 1:25 (it is corrupt to worship and serve "created things rather than the Creator").
46. Samyutta-Nikaya 56, quoted in A Buddhist Bible, ed. Dwight Goddard (Boston: Beacon 1994), p. 33.
47. Ibid.
48. Anguttara-Nikaya III. 33, quoted in Ibid. at p. 31.
49. Wallis Budge, *Egyptian Religion* (1899, reprint New York: Barnes & Noble 1994), pp. 141-42.
50. Ibid.
51. Ibid., p. 143.
52. The *Egyptian Book of the Dead*, E. A. Wallis Budge, trans. (Mineola: Dover 1967), Chapter 125.
53. S. G. F. Brandon, *The Judgment of the Dead* (New York: Scribners 1967), pp. 158-60.
54. Ibid.
55. *The Wisdom of China and India*, Lin Yutang ed. (New York: Random House 1942), p. 846.
56. Ibid.
57. Ibid., p. 853-54.
58. Ibid., p. 848.
59. Agamemnon lines 1560-64 in *Aeschylus*, David Grene and Richmond Lattimore eds., H. W. Smyth, trans. (University of Chicago Press 1960).
60. *The Wisdom of China and India*, Lin Yutang ed. (New York: Random House 1942), p. 846.

61. Ibid., pp. 801-02.
62. Ibid., p. 802.
63. Plato, Phaedo in Plato, *The Collected Dialogues*, Edith Hamilton and Huntington Cairns ed. (Princeton University Press 1989), p. 63.
64. Ibid., p. 89.
65. Ibid., p. 95.
66. Cicero, The Republic, Book III, Niall Rudd, trans. (Oxford: Oxford University Press 1998), p. 68.
67. Ibid., p. 69.
68. Ibid.
69. *Golden Sayings of Epictetus*, Hastings Crossley, trans. (Danbury: Grolier 1988), p. 140.
70. Ibid., p. 129.
71. Ibid., p. 134.
72. Ibid., p. 150.
73. Ibid., p. 169.
74. Ibid.
75. Quoted in Introduction, David Hume, *A Treatise of Human Nature* (London: Penguin 1969), p. 7.
76. Ibid., p. 507.
77. Ibid.
78. Ibid., p. 509.
79. Ibid.
80. Ibid., p. 523.
81. Ibid., p. 526.
82. Ibid., p. 522-24.
83. Immanual Kant, *Critique of Practical Reason* II, Conclusion (1788).

84. Immanual Kant, *Metaphysics of Morals*, Thomas Abbott, trans. (New York: Modern Library 2001), p. 187.
85. Ibid., p. 164.
86. Ibid., p. 165.
87. Immanual Kant, *Religion Within the Limits of Reason Alone*, Theodore Greene and Hoyt Hudson, trans. (New York: Harper 1960), p. 90.
88. Ibid., p. 91.
89. Ibid.
90. E. Harrison Clark, *All Cloudless Glory* (Washington D.C.: Regnery 1995), p. 252.
91. Ibid., p. 386.
92. Ibid., p. 410.
93. Washington's First Inaugural Address, in *Our Sacred Honor*, William J. Bennett ed. (Nashville: Broadman & Holman 1997), p. 382.
94. Ibid.
95. Letter to Henry Lee, September 22, 1788, quoted in *Maxims of George Washington*, John Schroeder ed. (Mount Vernon Ladies Ass'n 1989), p. 145.
96. Clark, *All Cloudless Glory*, p. 186.
97. Schiller, *Resignation* (1786), st. 19.
98. Schiller, *Wallenstein's Death* (1798), I, 7, 32.
99. Mark E. Neely, Jr., *The Last Best Hope of Earth* (Harvard University Press 1993), p. 158.
100. Ibid.
101. Quoted in William J. Federer, *America's God and Country* (Coppell: Fame Publishing 1994), p. 382.

102. David Herbert Donald, *Lincoln* (New York: Simon & Schuster 1995), p. 354.
103. Ibid., p. 515.
104. Ibid.
105. Quoted in *America's God and Country*, p. 383.
106. Ibid., pp. 389-90.
107. Jerome Kagan, *The Nature of the Child* (New York: Basic Books 1994) p. 131.
108. Ibid., p. 129.
109. Ibid., p. xxiii.
110. Ibid., p. xxiv.
111. Ibid., pp. 131, 152.
112. Ibid., p. 131.
113. Ibid., pp. 131-32.
114. Ibid., p. xxiii.
115. Ibid.
116. Matthew 22:37-40.
117. Deuteronomy 5:7-21.
118. Matthew 5:21-22.
119. Matthew 5:27-28.
120. See Matthew 23:23-26 (hypocrites appear outwardly good, but are inwardly greedy and self-indulgent).
121. Matthew 23:27-28.
122. Proverbs 27:19 ("As water reflects a face, so a man's heart reflects the man").
123. 1 Samuel 16:7 ("Man looks at the outward appearance, but the LORD looks at the heart").
124. Proverbs 21:2.

125. Galatians 6:7 ("A man reaps what he sows").

126. Proverbs 12:14.

127. Psalm 9:16.

128. See Psalm 10, where David expresses frustration with the success of the wicked. Many of the 150 Psalms have the same theme.

129. 1 Corinthians 4:5 (on judgment day, God "will bring to light what is hidden in darkness and will expose the motives of men's hearts"); Matthew 12:36 (we will have to account for every idle word we have spoken); Revelation 20:12 (people will be judged "according to their works").

130. Psalm 96:10-13 (God will judge the world in truth and equity).

131. Ernest Becker, *The Structure of Evil* (New York: Macmillan 1968), pp. 141-42.

132. Ibid., p. 300.

133. Ibid., p. 331.

134. Becker, *Escape From Evil* (New York: Macmillan 1975), pp. xvii-xviii.

135. Plato, *Laws in The Collected Dialogues of* Plato, E. A. Taylor, trans. (Princeton: Princeton University Press 1996), p. 1318.

136. Ibid.

137. Ibid.

138. Ibid.

139. Plato, *Republic in Collected Dialogues*, Paul Shorey, trans., p. 799.

140. Laws, p. 1320.

141. Ibid.

142. A *Source Book in Chinese Philosophy,* Wing-Tsit Chan, trans. (Princeton University Press 1963), p. 129.
143. Ibid.
144. Ibid., p. 128.
145. Ibid.
146. Seneca, *Moral Essays,* Volume 1, John Bascre, trans. (Harvard University Press 1963), p. 143.
147. Ibid., p. 321.
148. Seneca, *Letters to Lucilius,* Section 41.
149. Ibid., Section 22.
150. Plutarch on *Love, The Family, and The Good Life,* Moses Hadas, trans. (New York: Mentor 1957), p. 177.
151. Plutarch, *Moralia,* Volume 2, Frank Cole Babbitt trans. (Cambridge: Harvard University Press 1962), p. 35.
152. Ibid., Vol. 6, p. 5.
153. Francis duc de La Rochefoucauld, *Maxims, Introduction* (London: Penguin 1979), p. 14.
154. Ibid., p. 56.
155. Ibid., p. 72.
156. Ibid., p. 47.
157. Ibid., p. 60.
158. Ibid., p. 70.
159. Ibid., p. 42.
160. Ibid., p. 50.
161. Ibid., p. 52.
162. *The Autobiography of Benjamin Franklin* (New Haven: Yale University Press 1964), p. 155.

163. Ibid., p. 159. Arguably, Franklin did not achieve the second from last virtue either!

164. Ibid., p. 158.

165. William Blackstone, *Commentaries on the Laws of England*, Vol. 1 (Chicago: University of Chicago 1979), p. 40.

166. Ibid.

167. Ibid.

168. Ibid., p. 41.

169. Ibid.

170. Adam Smith, *Wealth of Nations* (Washington D.C.: Regnery 1998), p. 152.

171. Ibid., p. 389.

172. Ibid.

173. Ibid.

174. Adam Smith, *The Theory of Moral Sentiments* (Washington D.C.: Regnery 1997), pp. 63-64.

175. *Wealth of Nations*, p. 513.

176. Johann Wolfgang von Goethe, *Maxims and Reflections* (London: Penguin 1998), p. 92.

177. Ibid., p. 13.

178. Peter Eckermann, *Conversations with Goethe* (New York: Da Capo 1998), p. 324.

179. Ibid.

180. Ibid.

181. Quoted in *Viking Book of Aphorisms* (New York: Barnes & Noble Books 1993), p. 21.

182. *The Federalist* (Birmingham: Legal Classics Library 1983), p. 118.

183. Ibid., pp. 117-18.

184. Ibid., p. 118.
185. *The Portable Jung*, Joseph Campbell ed., R. F. C. Hull, trans. (London: Penguin Books 1971), p. 145.
186. Quoted in A *Dictionary of Quotations*, A. Norman Jeffares and Martin Gray, eds. (Harper Collins 1995), p. 368.
187. Richard Alexander, *The Biology of Moral Systems* (Hawthorne: Aldine de Gruyter 1987), p. 128.
188. Ibid.
189. Ibid.
190. Ibid., p. 142.
191. Robert Wright, *The Moral Animal* (New York: Vintage Books 1995), p. 13.
192. Ibid.
193. Ibid., p. 281.
194. October 23, 1997, *Wall Street Journal* at A14.
195. Ibid.
196. The one exception is Jesus, who the New Testament records was without sin (2 Corinthians 5:21). The significance of his moral purity is examined later in this book.
197. Genesis 20:2.
198. Exodus 2:12.
199. 1 Kings 11:1-11.
200. Isaiah 6:5. Isaiah said that the whole human race, like sheep, have all gone astray. (Isaiah 53:6)
201. Mark 14:66-72. Peter once asked Jesus not to associate with him, because "I am a sinful man!" (Luke 5:8)
202. Acts 8:3; 1 Corinthians 15:9. Paul considered himself "the worst of sinners." (1 Timothy 1:15)

203. Psalm 51:5.
204. Psalm 51:1-4.
205. Matthew 23:13-29.
206. Luke 18:14.
207. John 9:41.
208. *Harper Collins Dictionary of Religions*, Jonathan Z. Smith, ed. (New York: Harper Collins 1995), p. 498.
209. *World Religions* (New York: Simon & Schuster Macmillan 1987), pp. 335-36.
210. Ibid.
211. Qur'an 9:60. Note that the Qur'an is organized as a single book with 114 chapters.
212. Qur'an 4:7-25.
213. Qur'an 11:112.
214. Qur'an 11:5.
215. Qur'an 17:25-29.
216. Qur'an 2:262-64.
217. Qur'an 43:80.
218. Qur'an 17:14.
219. Qur'an 18:19.
220. Qur'an 101:6-11.
221. Qur'an 7:8.
222. Qur'an 7:9.
223. Qur'an 18:104.
224. A *Buddhist Bible*, Dwight Goddard ed. (Boston: Beacon Press 1994), p. 33.
225. Ibid., pp. 34-41.
226. Ibid., p. 42.

227. Ibid., pp. 42-43.
228. Ibid., p. 43.
229. Ibid., p. 45.
230. Ibid., pp. 45-47.
231. Ibid., pp. 47-55.
232. Ibid., pp. 55-60.
233. *Oxford Dictionary of World Religions*, John Bowker ed. (Oxford University Press 1997), p. 415.
234. Guru Granth, quoted in *Eerdman's Handbook to the World's Religions* (Grand Rapids: Eerdmans 1994), p. 204.
235. *Oxford Dictionary of World Religions*, p. 831.
236. *Harper Collins Dictionary of World Religions*, p. 768.
237. *The Compact Guide to World Religions*, Dean Halverson ed. (Minneapolis: Bethany 1996), pp. 165-66.
238. *Oxford Dictionary of World Religions*, John Bowker ed. (Oxford University Press 1997), p. 892.
239. *World Religions* (New York: Simon & Schuster Macmillan 1998), p. 174.
240. *Oxford Dictionary of World Religions*, p. 646.
241. *Religious Traditions of the World*, H. Byron Earhart ed. (Harper San Francisco 1993), p. 1151.
242. *Oxford Dictionary of World Religions*, p. 650.
243. *Bhagavad-Gita*, Swami Prabhavananda and Christopher Isherwood, trans. (Barnes & Noble 1995), p. 28.
244. *Oxford Dictionary of World Religions*, pp. 209-10.
245. Lyall Watson, *Dark Nature* (New York: Harper Collins 1995), p. 165.
246. Ibid., p. 255.

247. Ibid., p. 167.
248. Edward Evans-Pritchard, *Nuer Religion* (Clarendon 1956), pp. 4, 13.
249. Ibid., pp. 16-19.
250. Ibid., pp. 272-80.
251. Genesis 4:3-7.
252. Genesis 4:8.
253. Exodus Chapters 7—10.
254. Exodus Chapters 11—12.
255. Exodus 12:1-30.
256. Exodus 12:31-42.
257. Leviticus 16:10.
258. Leviticus 16:7-19.
259. Psalm 99:1.
260. Leviticus 16:20-26.
261. Isaiah 1:4.
262. Isaiah 1:11.
263. Isaiah Chapter 9.
264. Isaiah Chapter 53.
265. John 1:19-24.
266. Matthew 3:11-12.
267. John 1:29.
268. John 1:1-18.
269. Luke 3:23.
270. Luke Chapters 22—23.
271. Matthew 28; Mark 16; Luke 24; John 20—21.
272. Ibid.
273. See Matthew 9:13.
274. Luke 18:9-14.

Bibliography

Aquinas, Thomas. *Summa Theologiae*. Westminster: Christian Classics, 1989.

Athanasius. *On the Incarnation*. Crestwood: St. Vladimir's Seminary Press, 1996 reprint.

Augustine. *Confessions*. Franklin Center: Franklin Library, 1982.

Barbour, Ian G. *Religion and Science*. San Francisco: HarperCollins, 1997.

Barrow, John D. and Frank J. Tipler. *The Anthropic Cosmological Principle*. Oxford: Oxford University Press, 1986.

Brandon, S.G.F. *The Judgment of the Dead*. New York: Scribners Publishing, 1967.

Budziszewski, J. *The Revenge of Conscience*. Dallas: Spence Publishing, 1999.

Carroll, Vincent and David Shiflett. *Christianity on Trial*. San Francisco: Encounter Books, 2002.

Chesterton, G. K. *Orthodoxy*. New York: Image Books, 1990 reprint.

Clark, David K. and Norman L. Geisler. *Apologetics in the New Age*. Grand Rapids: Baker Book House, 1990.

Clark, David K. *Dialogical Apologetics*. Grand Rapids: Baker Book House, 1993.

Clark, Kelly James. *Philosophers Who Believe*. Downers Grove: Intervarsity Press, 1993.

Coward, Harold. *Life After Death in World Religions*. Maryknoll: Orbis Publishing, 1997.

Davies, Paul. *The Mind of God*. New York: Simon and Schuster, 1992.

Dawkins, Richard. *The Selfish Gene*. Oxford: Oxford University Press, 1976.

Degler, Carl. *In Search of Human Nature*. New York: Oxford University Press, 1991.

Dembski, William A. *Intelligent Design*. Downers Grove: Intervarsity Press, 1999.

Denton, Michael J. *Nature's Destiny*. New York: Free Press, 1998.

Eliade, Mircea. *Patterns in Comparative Religion*. London: Sheed and Ward Publishing, 1958.

Fuchs, Joseph. *Natural Law*. New York: Sheed and Ward Publishing, 1965.

Green, Ronald M. *Religious Reason*. New York: Oxford University Press, 1978.

Hume, David. *A Treatise of Human Nature*. London: Penquin Books, 1969 reprint.

Kennedy, D. James and Jerry Newcombe. *What if Jesus Had Never Been Born?* Nashville: Thomas Nelson, 1994.

Kevan, Ernest. *Moral Law.* Phillipsburg, NJ: P & R Publishing, 1991.

Kreft, Peter. *Back to Virtue*. San Francisco: Ignatius Press, 1992.

Kulandran, Sabapathy. *Grace in Christianity and Hinduism.* London: Lutterworth Press, 1994.

Lewis, C. S. *The Abolition of Man*. New York: Macmillan Publishers, 1978 reprint.

Lewis, C. S. *Mere Christianity.* New York: Touchstone Publishing, 1996 reprint.

Lippmann, Walter. *A Preface to Morals*. New York: Macmillan Publishers, 1929.

Little, Paul. *Know Why You Believe*. Downers Grove: Intervarsity Press, 1988.

Lovejoy, Arthur O. *Reflections on Human Nature*. Baltimore: Johns Hopkins University Press, 1961.

Moreland, J. P. *The Creation Hypothesis*. Downers Grove: Intervarsity Press, 1994.

Myers, David G. *The Inflated Self.* New York, Seabury Press, 1980.

Pearcey, Nancy R. and Charles B. Thaxton. *The Soul of Science.* Wheaton: Crossway Books, 1994.

Plantinga, Cornelius, Jr. *Not the Way It's Supposed to Be*. Grand Rapids: Eerdmans Publishing, 1995.

Polkinghorne, John. *The Faith of a Physicist*. Princeton, NJ: Princeton University Press, 1994.

Ross, Hugh. *The Creator and the Cosmos*. Colorado Springs: Navpress, 2001.

Schroeder, Gerald L. *Genesis and the Big Bang*. New York: Bantam, 1992.

Sproul, R. C. *Reasons to Believe*. Grand Rapids: Zondervan Publishing House, 1978.

Strobel, Lee. *The Case for Christ*. Grand Rapids: Zondervan Publishing House, 1998.

Strobel, Lee. *The Case for Faith*. Grand Rapids: Zondervan Publishing House, 2000.

Watson, Lyall. *Dark Nature*. New York: HarperCollins Publishers, 1995.